YORK N

General Editors: Professor A.N. Jeffares (*University of Stirling*) & Professor Suheil Bushrui (*American University of Beirut*)

Anne Brontë

THE TENANT OF WILDFELL HALL

Notes by Hana Sambrook

MA PH D (EDINBURGH)

LONGMAN
YORK PRESS

YORK PRESS
Immeuble Esseily, Place Riad Solh, Beirut.

LONGMAN GROUP LIMITED
Longman House,
Burnt Mill,
Harlow,
Essex

First published 1984
Second impression 1986
ISBN 0 582 79256 8
Produced by Longman Group (FE) Ltd
Printed in Hong Kong

Contents

Part 1

Introduction

The life of Anne Brontë

Anne Brontë was born on 17 January 1820 at Thornton, a suburb of Bradford, the large industrial centre of Yorkshire. Her father, the Rev. Patrick Brontë was the son of a peasant farmer in Northern Ireland, while her mother, formerly Miss Maria Branwell, came from a prosperous merchant family in Penzance, Cornwall. The Branwells were devout Methodists, followers of the great preacher John Wesley (1703–91). At this time the Methodists had not yet broken away from the Church of England to form a separate, more strictly Protestant sect, and so there was no difficulty about Maria's marriage to an Anglican clergyman.

While Anne was still only a tiny baby, the family moved to Haworth where Mr Brontë was appointed curate. It was not a well-paid post, and the family had always to live modestly.

Haworth was a very different place from Thornton; it was a small manufacturing village climbing steeply up towards the moorland, the beautiful but wind-swept and desolate 'pathless moor' of Anne Brontë's 'Verses by Lady Geralda'.

Not long after the Brontës moved to Haworth, Mrs Brontë fell seriously ill with cancer. There were six children in the family, the oldest eight years old and Anne, the youngest, still a baby. In this desperate situation Mrs Brontë's sister, Miss Elizabeth Branwell, came up from Cornwall to nurse her. Mrs Brontë died in September 1821, and her sister felt it her duty to stay on and look after the children. Being the youngest, Anne was under Miss Branwell's particular care, all the more so as she was delicate and was kept at home a good deal.

In spite of Miss Branwell's strict Methodism it would be a mistake to see the Brontës' childhood in dark colours only. The children were kept busy, with their lessons, with helping round the house, and there was the vicarage garden to play in, as well as the moor. Their upbringing does not seem to have been unduly strict by contemporary standards, and there were no hardships when it came to food and warmth. (When reading *The Tenant of Wildfell Hall* you may notice the careful descriptions of domestic interiors, of tables spread with good simple food, of cheerful warm fires, all of which feel entirely real and convincing.)

The first change in the children's lives came when Maria and

Elizabeth, the two eldest children, were sent away to boarding-school, first for a short time to Crofton Hall School, and then to Cowan Bridge Clergy Daughters' School at Kirby Lonsdale in Cumbria. Presumably the first reports of the school were satisfactory, because Charlotte joined her two sisters there, followed by Emily. It is now generally assumed that Cowan Bridge School served Charlotte as the model of Lowood Institution in *Jane Eyre*. Charlotte said later that insufficient diet, bad air and water were responsible for the high mortality among the pupils from any infection that came to the school.

The two elder Brontës, Maria and Elizabeth, were among the victims of the school's deficiencies. In February 1825 Maria was sent home 'in ill health' and died at Haworth in May. At the end of the same month Elizabeth came home, also because of 'ill-health', and died soon afterwards. Both sisters were buried in Haworth churchyard, beside their mother. (If you find a photograph of Haworth churchyard in an illustrated biography of the Brontës, you will see that the parsonage overlooks the churchyard. We can well imagine the constant reminder of the deaths this proximity must have been.)

It was natural that the thoughts of the children in this clerical household should have turned to the aftermath of death—redemption or damnation. Aunt Branwell was a devout Methodist, and this strict sect laid much emphasis on the question of salvation. Though the Wesleyan Methodists upheld the doctrine of redemption for all, and rejected the Calvinist belief in predestination for either salvation or damnation, Anne, who spent much time in her aunt's company, must have heard enough of this cruel belief to be haunted by the terror of damnation, even as a child. Listen to these lines from her poem 'Self-communion', written in 1847:

I see, far back, a helpless child,
Feeble, and full of causeless fears,
Simple and easily beguiled
    To credit all it hears ...

(Remember this preoccupation with the doctrine of salvation when you read *The Tenant of Wildfell Hall*, and you will understand why Helen tries so desperately to reform Arthur.)

After their sisters' deaths Emily and Anne drew closer together, both enjoying long walks on their beloved moor. In these, their love of nature grew, but while Emily's became a strange cosmic passion, for Anne the love of nature went with love of animals, of the small moorland flowers. In *The Tenant of Wildfell Hall* it is the loving observation of small details in nature that attracts the reader's attention.

At this time Mr Brontë, naturally enough following the loss of two children, kept the remaining four at home. The period 1826 to 1831 was a happy time for the little Brontës, a time of well-established routine of regular family prayers, regular household tasks, regular lessons with their father.

Mr Brontë, himself an author on a very humble scale (of poems and moral tales), subscribed to several newspapers as well as to literary periodicals, and was in the habit of reading from them to his children. The children obviously absorbed the political information from the newspapers and used it in creating their famous imaginary states. The story of the wooden toy soldiers given to Branwell by his father, which inspired these fantasies, is well known. What began as children's plays, such as many children delight in acting, grew into the 'Great Glass Town' cycle and then into the chronicles of two separate states. Branwell and Charlotte created Angria, a kingdom on the West Coast of Africa, and Anne and Emily had their Gondal, an island in the Pacific. The habit of writing became established through these chronicles—and so did the habit of keeping their writing secret. Emily and Anne kept up their Gondal writing well into adulthood, and in many of their poems the sisters speak through various Gondal characters.

This pleasant life came to an end when in 1831 Charlotte went to another school, Roe Head, first as a pupil and later as a teacher. A free place was offered to one of her sisters, and Emily joined her at the school. At about this time Branwell left home to study art in London; his story of failure began here, for he never actually attended the Royal Academy Schools.

Meanwhile Anne was left alone at home, though not for long. Emily was miserable at school, and so Anne was sent to Roe Head instead. She went quite willingly; unhappy about being so totally dependent on her father, she was determined to equip herself to earn her living. In spite of her gentleness and timidity she had a good deal of determination and moral courage in her nature; of all the girls she was the one to work away from home the longest, however miserable she was in her posts.

Her two years at school were not a happy time for Anne. In the end she fell seriously ill, and during her illness she suffered a religious crisis as well; in her weak physical state all the old childish terrors of the burden of sin and damnation came crowding in on her. She found help in the person of a clergyman who visited her during her illness. He was a minister of the Moravian Church, a small religious sect originating in Bohemia, which professed an altogether gentler kind of Protestantism, a doctrine of redemption through faith and divine love. This teaching did much to restore Anne's spirits and enabled her to recover from her illness. But she soon fell ill again, with what looked alarmingly like the onset of tuberculosis. Acting with commendable swiftness, her father brought her home.

Once she had regained her health, Anne decided to look for a post as governess. She succeeded in finding a situation with Mr and Mrs Ingham of Blake Hall at Mirfield in Yorkshire, a young couple with five children. She was very miserable at Blake Hall. She found herself unable to control the children or to gain their affections, and her sensitivity to the peculiar position of a governess, theoretically equal to her employers because she was a 'lady' and yet treated by them as their social inferior, made her task even more difficult. It is usually accepted that the odious Bloomfield family in Anne's first novel, *Agnes Grey*, was modelled on the Inghams. But the dislike she felt towards the Inghams was reciprocated, and at Christmas 1839 they dismissed her.

She stayed at home at Haworth for a year, as did both her sisters. During this tranquil year she may have fallen in love with her father's curate, William Weightman, a cheerful, outgoing young man with an easy social manner and a kind heart for the poor. There are a few poems of hers that indicate something of the sort, and some family stories of attentions paid, valentines sent, all the permitted indications of affection of the early Victorian period.

Evidently, however, no understanding had been reached, as in March 1841 Anne left home for another post as governess, this time with Mr and Mrs Robinson at Thorp Green, near York. Here she found the children amenable to her teaching and willing to accept her moral guidance. As is clear from her fiction, Anne's moral sense was very strong, and in her heart she condemned her employers for failing to impart to their children any moral precepts whatever. Nonetheless, when her brother Branwell, by now a drifter and a sad failure, was dismissed from his post as a railway clerk for carelessness, she persuaded Mr Robinson to engage him as tutor to his son.

This act of kindness had disastrous consequences. The facts of the matter are inevitably unclear, as there would have been a lot of covering up if the story was true, but it appears that Branwell embarked on a flirtation with Mrs Robinson, and however far the affair did or did not go, he was dismissed by Mr Robinson for behaviour 'bad beyond expression'. From that time on Branwell's decline through drink and drugs (he became an opium addict) was swift and relentless. It seems likely that Anne was aware of what was happening; she resigned from her post a few months before Branwell's dismissal.

Once more the young Brontës were all at home, but this time there was no happiness at the parsonage. Their Aunt Branwell died while Anne was still at Thorp Green (and so did the Rev. William Weightman, a victim of a typhus epidemic). With Miss Branwell dead and Branwell a drunkard, there was an end to the girls' dream of setting up a school together and so gaining their release from the subservient positions they so detested. One of them was needed at home to look after their father, and in any case how could they set up a school encumbered by the presence of their drunken brother?

Their misery was lifted when Charlotte accidentally discovered some of Emily's poems and realised their high quality. From this realisation came the idea of publishing jointly poems by all three sisters. In May 1846 the little volume of *Poems, by Currer, Ellis and Acton Bell* was published by a small London firm of Aylott and Jones, at the authors' own cost. The choice of male-sounding pseudonyms was deliberate, as the sisters thought there would be too much prejudice against women writers.

The volume of poems (which included twenty-one by Anne) was quite well received by critics, though inevitably poems by unknown authors proved an unsaleable commodity even in that poetry-reading age.

The importance of the *Poems* lay in the volume's alerting its authors to the possibility of a literary career, not in verse but in fiction—a natural development from those chronicles of their childhood. After several disappointments they at last found a publisher. In October 1847 Messrs Thomas Newby of London accepted Emily's *Wuthering Heights* and Anne's *Agnes Grey*, but turned down Charlotte's *The Professor*. That Charlotte tried her luck with Smith Elder, was encouraged to submit *Jane Eyre* instead of *The Professor*, and found herself—still as Currer Bell—a celebrity almost overnight, is one of the famous success stories of literary history. The publication of *Wuthering Heights* and *Agnes Grey* (the latter, oddly, as Volume III of *Wuthering Heights*) followed a few months later, but without quite achieving the success of *Jane Eyre*.

The Tenant of Wildfell Hall came out in 1848, and was an instant success of a certain kind. Reading the novel today we may find it hard to understand the fact that nineteenth-century critics denounced it for its 'coarseness' and for 'morbid revelling in scenes of debauchery', while the reading public devoured the novel for those very scenes.

Anne felt such criticism very deeply, and in the Preface to the second edition, which was published in the same year, she emphasised her high moral purpose in writing the book. She makes it quite clear that she wrote it as a warning against the evils of alcohol, and in her Biographical notice to a later edition Charlotte confirms that her sister had been inspired to write her novel by personal experience of an alcoholic decline.

Indirectly it was Anne's unscrupulous publisher, Newby, who forced the sisters to give up their anonymity. Trying to cash in on the greater popularity of *Jane Eyre*, Newby spread the rumour that Currer and Acton Bell were one and the same person, and he capped this deception by trying to sell the American rights of *The Tenant of Wildfell Hall* as a work by Currer Bell. Naturally Charlotte's publishers were rather annoyed at such sharp practice, suspecting their innocent author of taking part in it. The Brontës realised that the only way of convincing Smith Elder of their innocence was to travel to London and declare their identities and their innocence all at the same time. Charlotte and Anne undertook this journey, and we have ample evidence of the success of their mission and of the wonderful experience their visit to London as famous authors was for them.

These few exciting and happy days in July 1848 were soon over, and a sad time was coming yet again. In September 1848 Branwell died. The death certificate gave 'chronic bronchitis and marasmus' as cause of death, but really he died of the effect of years of heavy drinking and drug-taking. At his funeral Emily caught a chill, her condition grew worse, and by December she was dead.

Anne had been ailing for some time, and now it was clear that the two sisters, who had been inseparable as girls, would not be separated by death for very long. At her own wish Anne was taken to Scarborough, her favourite seaside resort in Yorkshire, which she had visited with the Robinsons, and there she died peacefully on 28 May 1849, of tuberculosis. She was twenty-nine years old. The doctor attending her declared that he had 'never seen such a death-bed'—so serene and calm was her acceptance of death.

The position of women in the nineteenth century

It is a curious fact that Anne Brontë's two novels touch on the two main aspects of the position of women in her time: the legal and economic dependence of married women on their husbands (*The Tenant of Wildfell Hall*) and the economic plight of single women which came about because their education did not train them to earn their own living (*Agnes Grey*). These remarks apply to women in the middle levels of society. The problems of the bold mill-girls in Mrs Gaskell's (1810–65) *North and South* (1855) are in a different category altogether, struggling as these women were to make a living in the new factories.

Legally, a woman ceased to exist as a person in her own right as soon as she married. On her marriage she was legally identified with her husband, and, a point to remember when reading Victorian novels, all her property automatically became his, except for any settlements by which a part of her property was expressly retained for her own use. The amount of the settlement depended on her husband's generosity and/or the skill of her family lawyers (we find Helen's uncle talking to her about settlements in Chapter 20).

The opportunities this law offered to unscrupulous fortune hunters is obvious: the plot of Wilkie Collins's (1824–89) famous novel *The Woman in White* (1860) hinges on exactly this legal helplessness of women. This situation continued until 1857, when a number of statutes were passed, changing the law and enabling a married woman to retain her rights to any property she possessed at the time of her marriage.

If the law saw women as incapable of managing their own property, it is understandable that this attitude should have been reflected in society's view of women. They were seen as helpless, unable to look after themselves, ignorant of the world, almost like children (in Chapter 25 of *The Tenant of Wildfell Hall* Arthur objects to Helen travelling alone, accompanied only by a footman and her maid!).

In turn society's view of women was reflected in the education provided for them. There was no question of their gaining professional qualifications beyond those proper to a wife (with a houseful of servants to carry out the hard task of running a comfortable household without any mechanical aids).

The frustration of such a life to any woman with a lively mind may well be imagined, and so may the appalling problems for any woman without private means who failed to marry or whose marriage turned out badly. Helen Huntingdon was fortunate (the point is stressed in the novel) in having a skill—her talent as a painter—which was socially acceptable for a lady and yet could be used to earn her a living.

In her other novel, *Agnes Grey*, Anne Brontë relates from personal experience the trials of a young lady (the term has a clearly defined special meaning in this context—a woman belonging to the gentry, above the level of tradesmen) who has to make her living by the only means open to her, as a governess:

> As none of the . . . ladies and gentlemen ever noticed me, it was disagreeable to walk beside them . . . . It was disagreeable, too, to walk behind, and thus appear to acknowledge my own inferiority; for, in truth, I considered myself pretty nearly as good as the best of them, and wished them to know that I did so . . . . (Chapter 13)

It is surprising that Anne Brontë should have chosen as her themes two feminist questions (for this is what they are in today's terms) since she was regarded as the gentlest, most retiring of the three sisters. Yet it was she who used her novels in a very direct way as vehicles of propaganda. As she herself says, in the opening words of *Agnes Grey*, 'All true histories contain instruction', and the instruction she imparts to us today is that women were unjustly treated by the society of her age.

Anne Brontë and her sisters

'The Brontës'—it is significant that they are commonly referred to in this way, almost as if they had no separate existence on their own—are regarded as a unique phenomenon in literature, and it is not surprising that this should be so. There have been other instances of writers joined by ties of blood or marriage: the pre-Raphaelite poet and painter Dante Gabriel Rossetti (1828–82) and his sister Christina (1839–94), the brothers Edmond (1822–96) and Jules de Goncourt (1830–70) in France, both novelists and men of letters, and the husband-and-wife team of Robert Browning (1812–89) and Elizabeth Barrett Browning (1806–61) and, among contemporary authors, the novelists C.P. Snow (1905–80) and his wife Pamela Hansford Johnson (1912–82), and Michael Holroyd (*b*. 1935) the biographer and his wife the novelist Margaret Drabble (*b*. 1939). But the case of the Brontës is different. There were three of them, all women novelists (in itself not so common in the early nineteenth century), and their sadly brief lives inevitably caught their readers' imagination.

Almost as a matter of course, once the habit is established of regarding them as a trio, the reader begins to look for parallels between their novels, to identify similarities and ignore differences, in order to make them and their work fit into a pattern.

It is true that they were close to each other from childhood. Living in a remote Yorkshire village, a clergyman's children, they were doubly set apart from the village children by their father's calling and by the fact that this calling made their father a gentleman. Social stratification was rigidly maintained in nineteenth-century England, and if the children had no social equals to play with within walking distance, they had to make do with each other. And make do they did; they had their lessons at home with their father until they were old enough to go to boarding-school, they played together, helped in the house, and they read together. In time they started their first attempts at creative writing together in their strange imaginary chronicles.

There were two such imaginary kingdoms, each created and maintained by two of the children, drawn closer to one another by this secret creativity. Emily and Anne were like twins, we are told. The same closeness could not be maintained between Charlotte and Branwell once they were older. The closeness of the ties of affection which bound the children together seems emphasised by the pattern of their lives. On glancing through their biographies the reader is bound to notice the recurrent phrase 'returned home'. Throughout their years away, first at school and then in their various posts, all the Brontës were forever coming back to Haworth, not just for one another's company, however dear, but for the bleak and beautiful landscape, for the wild moor where they spent so much of their childhood. This love of the place they knew best seems to have been almost a physical craving, a thing apart from family affections.

And yet, with all these strong ties binding them together, in spite of the evidence that they consulted each other on their work, the three Brontë sisters were quite different in themselves and in the novels they left us, and they are better served by their many admirers if they are seen as three novelists, each in her own right. Anne especially has suffered by constant comparisons with her sisters.

It has been suggested that had she not been a Brontë, sister to Charlotte and Emily, she would be quite forgotten now like many other lesser Victorian novelists (but re-discovered today, surely, by a feminist publishing house!). To suggest this is to do her less than justice. Her strength, which is peculiarly her own, lies in a sharp awareness of individuals—her picture of village society, of gentlemen farmers and their wives and families, is entirely convincing and charms while mocking gently. Her ear for dialogue surprises and impresses, while her vignettes of the Yorkshire countryside remind us in their freshness and accuracy of detail that Anne, while lacking the professionalism of her Helen Huntingdon, appears to have been a skilful draughtswoman. But beyond abilities of style she stands apart from her sisters by virtue of her strong sense of moral purpose, not to be found in Emily's *Wuthering Heights* nor in any of Charlotte's novels.

The qualities of her writing will be discussed in detail later (see Part 3, Commentary), but are mentioned here to add weight to the proposal that she and her sisters should be seen as three different writers, and their achievements judged by the standards peculiar to the type of novel each represents. They were close to one another during their lives, and it is impossible to recount even briefly the life of one without constant references to the others. But it should be possible and right to discuss each one's work entirely on its own merits.

A note on the text

The Tenant of Wildfell Hall, by Acton Bell, 3 vols, was published in London in 1848 by Thomas Cautley Newby. A second edition, substantially unaltered except for a preface by the author (usually omitted in modern editions) was published by Newby in the same year.

There are several modern editions of the novel, both hardcover and paperback. Details of these will be found in Part 5, Suggestions for further reading. As the reader may be using one of several editions, references to the text in these Notes are made by chapter, not by page number.

Part 2

Summaries
of THE TENANT OF WILDFELL HALL

A general summary

The first part of the novel (Chapters 1–15) is in the form of a long letter written by a young gentleman farmer, Gilbert Markham, to his brother-in-law. Markham lives on his farm, Linden-Car, with his widowed mother, his sister Rose and his young brother Fergus. A mysterious young widow, Mrs Graham, has just come to live at the half-derelict Wildfell Hall with her little son and her maid.

In spite of her efforts to remain aloof Mrs Graham is gradually drawn into the village society, and as Gilbert gets to know her better, they become friends. Gradually Gilbert finds himself attracted to her. She appears to be a professional painter, and there is some mystery about her. She seems to live in fear of being tracked down by someone, and is particularly anxious about her little boy, Arthur.

Village gossip soon links her with her landlord, Mr Lawrence, as he pays her rather frequent visits. The gossip turns slanderous: it is suggested that Mrs Graham is Mr Lawrence's mistress. Those chiefly responsible for spreading the gossip are Eliza Millward, daughter of the local clergyman, with whom Gilbert had been conducting a mild flirtation, and Jane Wilson, the ambitious daughter of a farmer, who had hoped to marry Mr Lawrence. The Rev. Mr Millward, a pompous and self-satisfied man, takes it upon himself to reprimand Mrs Graham. Gilbert hurries to comfort her. He declares his love for her, but Mrs Graham turns him down, promising to give him her reasons the following day. Gilbert leaves her, but, lingering in the garden on his way home, he overhears a conversation between Mrs Graham and Mr Lawrence which convinces him that the gossips were right about them.

He does not keep his appointment with Mrs Graham, and when he meets Mr Lawrence on the road to the local town, he strikes him with his riding-whip and leaves him lying injured on the ground.

Mrs Graham tells Gilbert that if he is prepared to believe the gossip, he does not deserve the explanation she was going to give him. They part in bitterness, but when Mrs Graham realises that Gilbert believed not the gossip but what he himself saw and heard (and misunderstood) she gives him her diary to read.

The second part of the novel (Chapters 16–44) consists of Mrs Graham's diary, starting in June 1821, six years earlier. Helen is a beautiful girl of eighteen, in London for her first season in society. She is accompanied by her uncle and aunt, Mr and Mrs Maxwell, who brought her up after her mother's death. Her father takes no interest in her at all.

In London Helen meets Arthur Huntingdon, a handsome young man-about-town. She is attracted to him, to the great displeasure of her aunt. Hoping to put an end to Helen's infatuation with Huntingdon, the Maxwells take her back to Staningley, their country home.

A few months later some friends of her uncle's arrive for the autumn partridge shooting, among them Huntingdon and his friend Lord Lowborough. Also in the party are two young girls, the handsome, flirtatious Annabella Wilmot and her timid cousin Milicent Hargrave. Huntingdon flirts with Annabella, and Helen is young enough to betray her distress at this. Huntingdon comforts her and declares his love for her. They become engaged, and so do Lord Lowborough and Annabella. Already Helen is made uneasy by some aspects of Huntingdon's character, but she is in love and full of confidence in her own ability to reform her future husband.

After their marriage, Helen and her husband go to live at Grassdale Manor, Huntingdon's country mansion. Soon Helen is forced to admit that her marriage has not turned out as she had expected. She finds her husband idle, shallow and pleasure-loving, and entirely lacking in moral principles. There is much he dislikes about her, too, chiefly her seriousness, her high principles and her deep religious faith. As Huntingdon is bored living in the country, he goes to London for months at a time, to lead a life of dissipation. Helen is left alone at Grassdale Manor, but in time she finds comfort in her new-born son.

During this time Milicent Hargrave marries Ralph Hattersley, one of Arthur Huntingdon's drinking companions. To help him to pass the time in the country, Huntingdon invites his friends over for the shooting. The guests are Lord Lowborough and Annabella, Hattersley and Milicent, and two men friends of Huntingdon's, Milicent's brother Walter Hargrave and Grimsby. Helen becomes friendly with Milicent's younger sister Esther who lives nearby. The men drink a lot, and the drunken scenes that take place disgust Helen.

Following the hints given to her by Walter Hargrave, Helen discovers that her husband and Lady Lowborough are lovers. She asks her husband for a separation, but he refuses. The Huntingdons continue to live in the same house, but they are now strangers to one another. Walter Hargrave visits them often and tries to press his attentions on Helen who repulses him.

Once more the usual visitors arrive, but the Lowboroughs' visit is cut short when Lord Lowborough discovers his wife's infidelity. Huntingdon is teaching his little son his own bad habits. Helen decides to leave her husband and take her son with her. As she has very little money, she resolves to use the one skill she has got—her painting—to earn her living. Huntingdon reads his wife's diary and so discovers her plans. He takes away all her money and jewelry and destroys her paintings and painting materials, thus making her virtually a prisoner in his house.

He engages a governess for little Arthur who turns out to be his mistress. Helen has already made new plans to escape, and now she carries them out. She, Arthur, and her faithful maid Rachel leave secretly and go to Helen's childhood home, Wildfell Hall, which her brother Frederick Lawrence has made habitable for her. There they live, Helen working at her painting and trying to keep the local people's curiosity at bay. There she meets Gilbert Markham. Here the diary stops abruptly.

In the third and last part of the novel (Chapters 45–53) Gilbert takes up the narrative where he had left off at the end of Chapter 15. Once he has read the diary he realises that Helen is blameless. He rushes to Wildfell Hall, and he and Helen declare their love for each other. Helen is, however, faithful to her marriage vows, and so they have to part, but they agree to write to each other in six months' time. In the meanwhile Gilbert has regular news of her through her brother Frederick who has forgiven him for attacking him in ignorance of the true relationship between brother and sister.

Huntingdon is thrown by his horse in the hunting field and seriously injured, and Helen goes back to nurse him. Her letters to her brother tell of his neglected, disorderly household and of Huntingdon's grave condition, made much worse by his alcoholism. After a drinking bout the internal wound caused by his fall turns gangrenous and he dies in great terror.

Now that Helen is a rich widow, Gilbert hesitates to approach her. Out of the blue the news reaches him, via the malicious Eliza Millward, that Helen is about to marry Walter Hargrave and that Lawrence has gone to attend the wedding. Gilbert leaves at once, and to his joy he finds that the bride and groom are Helen's friend Esther Hargrave and Lawrence himself. Pausing only to wish them joy, Gilbert rushes off to find Helen. She is staying at Staningley with her aunt, now widowed. On the way there Gilbert learns that Helen has inherited all her uncle's considerable wealth, and he feels that there is now an even deeper gulf between himself and Helen socially. He decides to see the house from a distance only and then return home. At the gates he meets Mrs Maxwell, Helen and little Arthur, and is persuaded to come up to the house. Once Helen realises that only her wealth has kept him away, the way is clear to their marriage and future happiness.

Detailed summaries

Chapter 1

The first section of the novel is in the form of a long letter from Gilbert Markham, a young gentleman farmer, to his brother-in-law Halford. It describes events that took place twenty years earlier, in October 1827. Gilbert returns home after a day's work on the farm. The whole family meets at the tea table: Gilbert, his widowed mother who spoils him, his pretty sister Rose and his lazy, mischievous young brother Fergus. The talk at tea is about the mysterious Mrs Graham, a beautiful young widow who has come to live with her little son and an old woman servant at the half-derelict Wildfell Hall. Mrs Markham and Rose pay her a visit and find her polite but reserved. Next Sunday, Gilbert watches her in church.

NOTES AND GLOSSARY:

-shire: presumably Yorkshire; it is a convention of the nineteenth-century novelists not to identify localities in their fiction

burying my talent: a reference to the Bible, Matthew 25:25

hiding my light under a bushel: an echo of the biblical phrase; see Matthew 5:15, 'Neither do men light a candle and put it under a bushel'

miry: muddy

surtout: (*French*) overcoat

sconce: head

not widow's weeds, but slightish mourning: at this time there were strict social rules as to mourning dress, depending on the degree of closeness to the dead person, and the length of time since the death

home-thrusts: in fencing, skilful hits; used to mean remarks that hurt as intended

retroussé: (*French*) upturned

'How doth the little busy bee': opening words of Isaac Watts's (1674–1748) moralising poem 'Divine Song'

Chapter 2

Out shooting with his dog, Gilbert walks past Wildfell Hall. Mrs Graham's little boy tries to climb the garden wall to see the dog. Gilbert catches him as he slips. Mrs Graham runs up and snatches the child from him. Annoyed, Gilbert goes away and visits the vicarage. He is flirting with the vicar's younger daughter, Eliza Millward.

NOTES AND GLOSSARY:

Linden-Car:	the name of Gilbert's farm
superannuated:	old
boxwood swan...castellated towers...gigantic warrior...lion:	these are examples of the art of topiary—the skilful trimming of shrubs into various fanciful shapes
Mahomet...mountain:	from Sir Francis Bacon's (1561–1626) *Essays*, 12, 'Boldness': 'If the hill will not go to Mahomet, Mahomet will go to the hill.'
Berlin wools:	fine wool in a variety of colours
tête-à-tête:	(*French*) intimate conversation between two people
Miss Millward:	the correct form of address for the older sister: the Christian name was omitted

Chapter 3

Mrs Graham visits the Markhams, bringing her little boy, Arthur, with her. She refuses the wine offered to her, and so does Arthur. She explains to the Markhams that she has brought him up to loathe the taste of it. An argument develops over her way of bringing up the child.

NOTES AND GLOSSARY:

mercurial:	active, quick
milksop:	an effeminate, weak man
natural corruptions:	an allusion to the belief that man was born sinful and can only be redeemed through God's grace
Miss Nancy:	an effeminate man

Chapter 4

The Markhams give a party to which all the neighbours are invited, including Mr Lawrence, the owner of Wildfell Hall, and Jane Wilson who would like to marry him. Mrs Graham is eagerly discussed as she is not present.

NOTES AND GLOSSARY:

laudanum:	alcoholic tincture of opium, freely available at that time, as its dangerous habit-forming properties were not yet fully understood

Chapter 5

Gilbert and Rose Markham pay a visit to Mrs Graham and are surprised to discover that she is a professional painter, and uses false initials to sign her pictures. The mystery surrounding her deepens; an unseen visitor, evidently a man, arrives, and Mrs Graham hastily leaves the room. In her absence Gilbert finds a portrait of a handsome, dissolute-looking man. When Mrs Graham returns, she appears angry at his discovery.

NOTES AND GLOSSARY:

trespassed too much upon the forehead: a low forehead was regarded as an indication of low intellect

Chapter 6

Gilbert grows more and more interested in Mrs Graham and contrives to meet her frequently on her walks. Mr Lawrence tries to warn him off.

NOTES AND GLOSSARY:

gibbous moon: moon at the interim stage between a half-moon and full moon

Chapter 7

Gilbert, his brother and sister, and Eliza call on Mrs Graham. They all agree to go on a picnic by the sea, as Mrs Graham very much wishes to paint a seascape. The picnic is a success, but Eliza now realises that Gilbert is attracted to Mrs Graham.

NOTES AND GLOSSARY:

lubberly: clumsy
acclivity: upward slope
sea-mews: seagulls
electric start: a shock
complacency: quiet pleasure

Chapter 8

Gilbert's friendship with Mrs Graham deepens. He orders from London a copy of Sir Walter Scott's *Marmion* which he hopes she will accept as a present. At first she refuses to take the book, but he convinces her that he will not presume on their friendship if she accepts.

NOTES AND GLOSSARY:

Marmion: a romantic narrative poem with a sixteenth-century background, by Sir Walter Scott (1771–1832). First published in 1808, *Marmion* remained popular for a very long time
morocco: fine goatskin leather

Chapter 9

Gilbert discovers that the ladies of the village are gossiping about Mrs Graham, and when his mother gives another little party for the neighbours, at which Mrs Graham and little Arthur are also present, he realises the seriousness of the gossip. Eliza, who is jealous, hints that Mrs Graham is Mr Lawrence's mistress and that he is the father of her little boy. Gilbert does not believe the gossip, but nevertheless he exchanges angry words with Mr Lawrence when the latter warns him yet again not to think of Mrs Graham.

NOTES AND GLOSSARY:

cambric: fine white linen fabric
optics: eyes
about the gills: in the face

Chapter 10

Gilbert calls on Mrs Graham and allows her to see that he is in love with her. He promises, however, not to mention his feelings to her again and continue as her friend only. On his way home he meets Mr Lawrence. They quarrel, but are interrupted by the vicar.

NOTES AND GLOSSARY:

pretty far gone: very much in love
plucked a ... bud: this motif of the rose recurs, again as a symbol, in Chapter 53
'You ... pony be—': the dash is used to indicate the omission of the swearword 'damned' according to the accepted convention

Chapter 11

Gilbert's friendship with Mrs Graham deepens, and they are now on first-name terms. Rose tells Gilbert that there is much scandalous gossip about Mrs Graham, and that it is spread chiefly by Eliza and Jane Wilson (who, having failed to attract Mr Lawrence, is now jealous of Mrs Graham). The vicar calls on the Markhams and tells them of his visit to Mrs Graham. He had felt it his duty to reprimand her and was quite startled to find that his visit angered her so much that she asked him to leave. Gilbert is furious at this officious impertinence on Mr Millward's part, and rushes off to see Mrs Graham.

NOTES AND GLOSSARY:

pastoral: relating to the clergyman's duty

Chapter 12

Gilbert finds Helen Graham very upset by the vicar's reprimands. Her evident unhappiness gives him the courage to declare his love for her and ask her to be his wife. She tells him that there are reasons why she cannot marry him, and promises to tell him everything the next day, as she is too upset to speak now. He leaves in a fever of excitement and passion and, having gone some distance, decides to return to Wildfell Hall in the hope of catching a glimpse of Helen from a distance. While he is standing in the garden, Helen comes out, accompanied by Mr Lawrence. They talk in such affectionate terms that Gilbert is quite convinced now of the truth of the scandalous gossip. He rushes home in a state of desperate unhappiness.

NOTES AND GLOSSARY:
disposed for ignition: arranged all ready for lighting
cast of a die: a throw in a game of dice
harvest moon: the full moon nearest to the autumnal equinox, which is generally very bright
venerable pile: a building of a very great age
couch of thorns: a metaphorical expression (more commonly 'a bed of thorns'), meaning an uncomfortable position

Chapter 13

Gilbert is deeply unhappy about Mrs Graham's treachery. To take his mind off his misery, he decides to go and see the farmer Robert Wilson, Jane's brother, on business. However, he finds Eliza there, visiting Jane. Both girls take this opportunity to tease Gilbert with much malice, knowing that he has stopped his visits to Mrs Graham. On his way home he sees Arthur with his mother, but ignores them.

NOTES AND GLOSSARY:
'Shall I, because a woman's fair': a line from 'The Lover's Resolution' by George Wither (1588–1667)
Cupid: the Greek god of love, usually represented as a boy armed with a bow and arrows. The pangs of love are his arrow wounds
discussion: here, consumption, eating
pursued the even tenor of my way: kept on walking

Chapter 14

The following day Gilbert rides to the local town on business. Mr Lawrence on his pony catches up with him and tries to talk in a friendly way. In a sudden fit of jealous rage Gilbert strikes him with his riding-whip, causing him to fall off his pony. On his return home Gilbert hears the news that Mr Lawrence has been thrown by his horse and slightly injured. Clearly Mr Lawrence does not intend to reveal the true cause of his fall.

NOTES AND GLOSSARY:
criminate: accuse

Chapter 15

Two days later Gilbert is busy supervising the harvest when Helen arrives and insists on speaking to him. She clearly assumes that he has been avoiding her because he believes the gossip about her. She now feels that he is unworthy of the explanation she was going to give him. The following day Gilbert goes again to Wildfell Hall, curious to know what Helen was going to tell him. They exchange bitter words, but then Helen realises that Gilbert believes not the gossip but what he himself had overheard in the garden. She hands him her diary and tells him to take it away and read it.

NOTES AND GLOSSARY:
Sir Humphry Davy: Davy (1778–1829) was a famous English chemist, the inventor of the miner's safety lamp

Chapter 16

The second part of the novel, Helen's diary, begins here. The diary goes back six years, to 1821. Helen has just returned to the country after her first season in London. (Young girls of well-to-do families were, and still are, brought to London for the 'season', a round of social engagements during which it was hoped that they would find a husband.) She lives with her uncle and aunt, Mr and Mrs Maxwell, the latter a strict, rather humourless lady, who is obviously not happy in her marriage. During her stay in London Helen refused an offer of marriage from Mr Boarham, a dull, respectable man many years her senior. She also met Arthur Huntingdon, a handsome young man with a reputation for wild living. Her aunt cautions her against marrying for good looks alone.

NOTES AND GLOSSARY:
Remember Peter: a biblical reference, to Matthew 26: 33–5. Peter made boastful promises of loyalty to Jesus which he broke that same night
the tempter: Satan

Boarham . . . Bore'em: a not particularly witty joke. Both names are of course pronounced the same way

physiognomist: one able to tell a person's character from his face

Chapter 17

Helen remembers a dinner party a few days after she met Mr Huntingdon. The host was Mr Wilmot, a rich, dissolute old rake. Among the guests were his handsome, flirtatious niece Annabella, and her quiet cousin Milicent Hargrave with whom Helen became friendly. After dinner Helen is pestered by her host and rescued by Mr Huntingdon who then engages her in a flirtatious conversation. It is clear that he knows quite well that Helen finds him attractive. Helen's aunt interrupts their talk and takes Helen home. She disapproves of Mr Huntingdon and is alarmed at Helen's confident assertion that she could reform him. Helen's uncle suffers from gout and is easily persuaded by his wife that they should all return to the country.

NOTES AND GLOSSARY:

to hand in: to lead into the dining-room on his arm

Vandyke: Sir Anthony Van Dyck (1599–1641), a Flemish portrait painter, fashionable at the English court

the place prepared for the devil and his angels: a curious euphemism for hell. The angels are of course the fallen angels

Chapter 18

Helen has settled down to her usual routine, but she cannot forget Arthur Huntingdon. Some months later, a party of her uncle's friends arrive for the autumn partridge shooting. Among them are Mr Wilmot, Mr Boarham, and Mr Huntingdon with his friend Lord Lowborough. Annabella and Milicent are also of the party. One evening after dinner Mr Huntingdon looks through the portfolio of Helen's drawings and finds there several drawings of himself. The following morning he finds yet another sketch which Helen, furious at his complacent laughter, throws on the fire. After this incident he ignores her and flirts with Annabella.

NOTES AND GLOSSARY:

ignis fatuus: (*Latin*) 'fatal fire', light on the marshes caused by the combustion of marsh gas, which leads travellers astray; a dangerous delusion

sotto voce: (*Italian*) in a low voice

Hebe: in Classical mythology the beautiful goddess of youth who attended on the gods

Chapter 19

Mr Huntingdon continues to ignore Helen. Annabella, an accomplished singer, sings a sad little song. Helen, miserable at Huntingdon's neglect, is so much affected by the sad song that she has to leave the room. Arthur Huntingdon follows her, comforts her and proposes to her. Helen's aunt enters, much displeased at what she sees.

NOTES AND GLOSSARY:

Farewell to thee?...: the words of the song are by Anne Brontë herself

Chapter 20

In the morning Helen has a serious conversation with her aunt who begs her to consider Mr Huntingdon's character and his reputation for dissolute living, but Helen is confident that she will be able to reform him. Her uncle (who acts also as her guardian as her father has taken no interest in her since her mother's death), gives his consent and the wedding is arranged to take place at Christmas.

NOTES AND GLOSSARY:

effulgence: brightness

a brand ... burning: see the Bible, Amos 4:11, 'ye were as a firebrand plucked out of the burning'

Blatant: in pronunciation this word is not unlike 'Leighton'. Huntingdon's humour, like Anne Brontë's, is not of the highest order

'What fellowship hath light...': a quotation from the Bible, 2 Corinthians 6:14–15

'If he hear not them...': a quotation from the Bible, St Luke 16:31

'The wicked shall be...': a quotation from the Old Testament, Psalm 9:17

'till he has paid the uttermost farthing': from the Bible, St Matthew 5:26

'if any man's work abide not the fire...': from the Bible, I Corinthians 3:15

'is able to subdue all things...': from the Bible, Philippians 3:21

'will in the fullness of time, gather together...': from the Bible, Ephesians 1:10

Nell: pet name for Helen

rules the roast: predominates

the matter of settlements: see Part 1, 'The position of women in the nineteenth century', p.10 above

Chapter 21

The news of the engagement is not well received by the others. Milicent and Annabella both express their surprise and doubt, while Huntingdon's friends blame him for breaking up their merry bachelor circle.

NOTES AND GLOSSARY:
Sir Herberts and Valentines: typical names of heroes of romances
'all for love or the world well lost': a quotation of the title of John Dryden's (1631–1700) play *All for Love, or The World well lost* (1678) which deals with the tragic love of Antony and Cleopatra

Chapter 22

Helen grows uneasy as she learns more of Huntingdon's character. He tells her boastfully of his evil influence on Lord Lowborough whom he encouraged to gamble away his fortune and take to drink. Lowborough fell seriously ill from the effects of excessive drinking, and when he recovered he decided to mend his ways and reform through marriage. It now seems that he will be successful in this, as he has fallen in love with Annabella. Arthur knows, however, that Annabella will marry Lord Lowborough for his title alone. Helen is appalled by the part Arthur has played in Lord Lowborough's sad tale. Her uneasiness increases when her maid hints at Arthur's unsavoury reputation. But Helen is in love and will not listen.

NOTES AND GLOSSARY:
boobies and bedlamites: fools and madmen
felo de se: (*Anglo-Latin*) suicide
because you're a peer: members of both the House of Commons and the House of Lords could claim immunity from arrest for debt. This privilege has now been abolished
skeleton at a feast: the Greek historian Plutarch (*c.* AD46–120) tells us in his *Moralia* that the Egyptians used to place a skeleton at a banquet table, to remind them of the nearness of death in the midst of pleasures
laudanum: see note to Chapter 4 above
ghost in Macbeth: in William Shakespeare's (1564–1616) *Macbeth* III.4 the ghost of the murdered Banquo appears to Macbeth at a banquet
media-via: (*Latin*) middle course, halfway between two extremes

ni-jamais-ni-toujours: (*French*) 'neither never nor always', avoiding the extremes
cachinnations: loud laughter

Chapter 23

Helen has now been married for two months and is the mistress of Grassdale Manor, the Huntingdon family mansion. In her diary she admits that her marriage has been a disappointment. Though Arthur loves her, she is only a toy to him, never to be taken seriously. She is also very aware of his selfishness, and his idle, pleasure-loving way of life.

NOTES AND GLOSSARY:
organ of veneration: the pseudo-science of phrenology was very popular in the early nineteenth century. It claimed to be able to diagnose a man's intellectual ability and character from the bumps on his head. There are several references to it in *Jane Eyre* as well
his one talent: see Matthew 25:14−29 for this parable of the misuse of natural gifts
'Who can eat ...': a quotation from the Bible, Ecclesiastes 2:25
'There is nothing better for a man ...': Ecclesiastes 2:24
'Rejoice, O young man ...': Ecclesiastes 11:9

Chapter 24

Arthur grows more and more bored with his idle life in the country. He and Helen quarrel, make it up and decide to go to London.

NOTES AND GLOSSARY:
letter-bag: in wealthy households the mail was collected and delivered to the house in a special bag for the use of that household alone

Chapter 25

Helen stays in London for a month and then returns to Grassdale Manor alone, by Arthur's wish. She is expecting a child, and is lonely without Arthur. In a letter he tells her that Milicent Hargrave is going to be married to Ralph Hattersley, a friend of his, a domineering, dissolute man. When Arthur returns at last, three months later, he is ill from the effects of his riotous living in London. Once he has recovered, he grows bored again, and decides to invite some friends to Grassdale Manor for the shooting.

NOTES AND GLOSSARY:
the needful: money
his old governor: his old father
quit the stage: die
'sweet regent of the sky': from W.J. Mickle's (1734–88) poem 'Cumnor Hall'

Chapter 26

The guests have arrived, among them Lord and Lady Lowborough. Lord Lowborough looks healthier and happier, but his wife seems to enjoy tormenting him by her flirtation with Arthur Huntingdon. Helen is not upset by this, as she feels that Arthur is simply indulging his vanity. They visit Mrs Hargrave, Milicent's mother, a hard, worldly woman, who, having made one daughter marry for money, is now hoping to do the same for her younger daughter Esther, a pretty, spirited girl, still quite young.

Chapter 27

Helen observes her husband in a rather intimate conversation with Lady Lowborough. She is angry at his behaviour while he tries to turn the matter into a joke and seems flattered by her jealousy. Helen warns him that he will lose her love if he persists. Lady Lowborough suggests that Arthur's behaviour was due to too much drink, and Helen pretends to be satisfied with this explanation.

NOTES AND GLOSSARY:
tête-à-tête: see note to Chapter 2 above
However we do praise ...: lines from Shakespeare's *Twelfth Night* II.4.32–5
curtain lecture: a scolding given by a wife to her husband in bed. The phrase refers to the curtains round a four-poster bed

Chapter 28

A year after her Christmas wedding Helen sees her marriage in a sober light, but she is happy in her new-born son.

The diary then skips another year. It is now 1823, and Helen's son is thriving. He is her only consolation as she now knows that there is no real sympathy between her and her husband who leaves her alone with her little boy at Grassdale for long periods at a time while he enjoys the dissipations of London.

Chapter 29

While living alone, Helen makes friends with Milicent's young sister Esther Hargrave. Their brother Walter, another member of Arthur's circle of friends, arrives during this time and begins to pay a good deal of attention to Helen, expressing his indignation at Arthur's neglect of her. His behaviour makes Helen uneasy.

NOTES AND GLOSSARY:
phaeton: a light open carriage

Chapter 30

At last Arthur returns, in a much worse state after his riotous life in London. He abuses the servants, is irritated by the baby and is drinking heavily. Gradually his health and his temper improve, and he is drinking less—a fact brought about by the influence of Walter Hargrave who is a constant visitor. But now the spring is approaching, and Helen knows that Arthur will leave her again for London.

NOTES AND GLOSSARY:
bathos: here, depth of degradation
repulsion: revulsion

Chapter 31

Arthur goes away again, and returns in his usual degraded state. Helen's father dies, but Arthur will not permit her to attend his funeral and see her brother. At the end of the summer Arthur's friends come to stay again: Lord and Lady Lowborough, Hattersley with Milicent and their baby daughter, Walter Hargrave and Grimsby, a coarse, violent man. Some rather unpleasant drunken scenes take place, but Lord Lowborough and Hargrave do not join in. Lady Lowborough's behaviour towards her husband seems much more affectionate and considerate.

NOTES AND GLOSSARY:
stiver: a Dutch penny; hence, any small coin
Sine as ye brew . . . : words of a Scots song ('As you brewed the ale, my fair maiden, remember that you must drink it'). The meaning is the same as in the proverb 'You made your bed, you lie on it'
pique: feeling of wounded pride
'In quietness and confidence shall be your rest': a misquotation of 'In quietness and confidence shall be your strength' from the Bible, Isaiah 30:15

fowls of heaven and lilies of the field: echoes of Matthew 6:26, 28, quite unsuitable in this context. Perhaps the misuse is intentional, to emphasise that Hattersley is drunk

'The light of the eye . . . ': from the Bible, Luke 11:34

have satisfaction: challenge to a duel

Chapter 32

Helen grows very fond of Milicent's young sister Esther. Both she and Milicent are very much afraid that Esther too will make an unhappy marriage. Milicent, however, feels that her husband is not as bad as Arthur Huntingdon and that he will reform one day. Hargrave asks to speak to Helen privately as he has 'bad news'. She refuses to listen.

NOTES AND GLOSSARY:

quit the stage . . . . close his accounts: die

old Trojan: (*slang*) good old fellow

'God be merciful to me a sinner': words from Luke 18:13

forgive his brother's trespasses: a mocking echo of the Lord's Prayer

Chapter 33

Helen overhears Grimsby and Hattersley grumbling about their host's change of heart due to a woman's influence, and she assumes that her good influence has won Arthur over at last. She is happy, and shows her happiness by affectionately embracing her husband who seems strangely taken aback. Her servant Rachel, however, tries to warn her against Lady Lowborough. Hargrave challenges her to a game of chess. As they play, the game assumes a strange duel-like character, and when Hargrave wins, Helen is frightened. He insists on telling her the 'bad news'. Her husband has been having an affair with Lady Lowborough, abetted by Grimsby. Helen goes out into the garden and finds her husband with Annabella. Unobserved by them, she sees and hears enough to convince her that Hargrave told her the truth. Later she confronts her husband, and while he admits his guilt, he refuses to set her free and return her fortune to her (in this he has the law on his side). Helen is forced to remain but she declares to her husband that from now on she will be his wife in name only.

Chapter 34

Helen makes it clear to Lady Lowborough that she knows about the affair, and requests her to leave as soon as possible. She promises, however, not to tell Lord Lowborough of his wife's infidelity.

Chapter 35

As her departure draws nearer Lady Lowborough grows bolder, flaunting her love for Arthur Huntingdon and mockingly boasting to Helen that her good influence alone has stopped his drinking. Hargrave feels free now to declare his love for Helen, but she rejects him. From the behaviour of Grimsby and Hattersley she realises that they assume that she has accepted Hargrave as her lover.

NOTES AND GLOSSARY:
sick with passion: sick with rage
go, and sin no more: these are the words spoken by Jesus to the
woman taken in adultery (see the Bible, John 8:11)

Chapter 36

Helen has now been married for three years. She and her husband live in the same house, but as total strangers. Huntingdon has started to drink again; he is spoiling his little son, partly out of boredom, and partly out of spite against Helen.

NOTES AND GLOSSARY:
soi-disant: (*French*) so-called, would-be
'that feareth the Lord...': a quotation from the Bible, Isaiah 50:10

Chapter 37

Little Arthur finds his sad mother rather poor company and turns increasingly to his indulgent father. Luckily Huntingdon leaves on a round of visits to his friends. Walter Hargrave takes this opportunity to pester Helen with his protestations of love, expecting her to yield now that she no longer loves her profligate husband. In the end, however, Helen succeeds in convincing him that she will never be his mistress.

Chapter 38

Helen has now been married for five years, and she is resolved to leave her husband. Huntingdon is entertaining his friends again, Lord and Lady Lowborough among them. Their visit is cut short, however, when Lord Lowborough discovers his wife's infidelity. He is distraught, but refuses to challenge Huntingdon to a duel, and resists the temptation to commit suicide.

NOTES AND GLOSSARY:
dews of agony: sweat

Chapter 39

Helen is strengthened in her resolve to leave her husband by his behaviour; he is now teaching his little son to drink and to swear. As she has no money of her own, Helen decides to work on improving her painting technique so as to be able to produce saleable pictures. She works in solitude while her husband amuses himself with his usual drinking companions, Walter Hargrave among them. Helen confides to Hargrave her plan to escape from Grassdale. He presses her passionately to entrust herself to him but she wards him off. Their struggle is witnessed by Grimsby. Huntingdon now accuses Helen of being Hargrave's mistress, but she defends herself and compels Hargrave to admit that he has not succeeded in winning her.

NOTES AND GLOSSARY:

moped: here, made dull and miserable

par parenthèse: (*French*, 'in brackets') in an aside

Chapter 40

Huntingdon reads his wife's diary and so discovers her plans. He destroys all her paintings and painting materials, and takes away all her money and jewels. Helen is now virtually a prisoner at Grassdale Manor.

NOTES AND GLOSSARY:

'He hath hedged me about . . . ': from the Bible, the Old Testament, Lamentations 3:7

'He hath filled me with bitterness . . . ': Lamentations 3:15

'But though He cause grief . . . ': Lamentations 3:32−3

'It is not the will of your Father . . . ': from the New Testament, Matthew 18:14

Chapter 41

Huntingdon has left again, confident that his wife cannot escape as she has no money. Helen sets to work on her son, to break him of all the bad habits, including the liking for alcohol, which he has learnt from his father. She has worked out another plan of escape: to ask her brother Frederick to make part of the old Hall where they lived as children, habitable again, and let her live there under an assumed name.

NOTES AND GLOSSARY:

tartar-emetic: a compound of potassium, antimony, carbon, hydrogen and oxygen, which induces vomiting

one who shall be nameless: the devil
younger sons: if, as very often happened, the family estate was
entailed, that is, inherited by the eldest son, the
younger ones were left without any property, and
therefore were not regarded as desirable husbands
cumberer of the ground: from the parable of the barren fig-tree in
Luke 13:7 – 'why cumbereth it the ground?'

Chapter 42

Huntingdon is still away. The Hattersleys are visiting Mrs Hargrave,
and Helen takes this opportunity to urge Hattersley to reform and to
treat his wife more kindly, which he promises to do.

NOTES AND GLOSSARY:
primed: stimulated by alcohol
worriting: (*dialect*) worrying, anxious

Chapter 43

Huntingdon returns and announces that he has engaged a governess
for Arthur, a Miss Myers. Helen learns through her maid Rachel that
the girl is her husband's mistress. This decides her: she writes to her
brother to get the Hall ready, packs her few belongings secretly, and,
taking Arthur and Rachel with her, leaves early one morning.

NOTES AND GLOSSARY:
was 'down of that ... governess': (*dialect*) disliked the new governess
fiddle: short for 'fiddlesticks', meaning 'nonsense'

Chapter 44

They travel by coach, Helen dressed in mourning and calling herself
Mrs Graham (her mother's maiden name), a young widow. Late at
night they arrive at the Hall and find that Helen's brother, Frederick
Lawrence, has had part of the Hall made ready for them. He cannot
visit his sister very often, as he is pretending to be her landlord, and no
relation of hers. Helen is still anxious, as she knows from her brother
that her husband is making every effort to find her, or rather to find his
son. The inquisitiveness of her present neighbours is causing Helen
some anxiety, and she decides to pay a few social calls and attend
church, in order to satisfy her neighbours' curiosity. In this way she
meets Gilbert Markham. Here the diary ends abruptly, as Helen has
obviously torn off the page on which she had written her impressions
of Gilbert, before lending him the diary.

NOTES AND GLOSSARY:
evergreens of preternatural forms: see note on 'boxwood swan . . . ',
          Chapter 2 above

Chapter 45

Now that Helen's diary has come to an abrupt end, the narrator is once more Gilbert Markham, continuing his long letter to Halford. He had spent most of the night reading the diary, and he is overjoyed to know that Helen is as free of blame as he had believed her to be. He hurries to Wildfell Hall to beg her forgiveness for having doubted her, while she in her turn asks him to forgive her for not having told him her story earlier.

Realising that she is still tied to her husband by her marriage vows, he is prepared to wait until her husband's death sets her free. Helen is determined to move to another part of the country, but they agree that Gilbert should write to her in six months' time. They embrace and part. Gilbert decides to call on Frederick Lawrence and ask his pardon for having attacked him. Naturally enough, Lawrence receives him rather coldly at first, but once he realises what Gilbert's motives had been, he forgives him and the two men part on friendly terms.

NOTES AND GLOSSARY:
descant upon: comment on them at length
adamant _n_: a hard substance; a diamond

Chapter 46

Gilbert would like to clear Helen's good name, but he fears that, if the true story were known, Eliza Millward might out of spite tell Huntingdon of his wife's whereabouts. He therefore remains silent. He visits Frederick Lawrence often, to have news of Helen, and the two men become friends. Gilbert warns Lawrence of Jane Wilson's true character. Lawrence is annoyed at first, but realises the truth of Gilbert's words, and acts accordingly.

NOTES AND GLOSSARY:
sensible: here, sensitive
rayless: cheerless

Chapter 47

Eliza Millward calls on the Markhams with the news that Mrs Graham has gone back to her husband. Gilbert hurries to see Lawrence and finds that this is so. Huntingdon had a fall in the hunting field and is very ill, and Helen has gone back to nurse him. Lawrence has heard from her since, and he lets Gilbert read her letter. She found her husband ill and neglected, and the house in disorder. She has set the household to rights again, and is slowly nursing her husband back to health. His constitution has been greatly damaged by his dissipated habits, and the recovery is slow.

NOTES AND GLOSSARY:
monomania: an obsessive interest in one subject only
intelligence: information
casting her pearls before swine: see Matthew 7:6, 'Neither cast ye your pearls before swine', words from Jesus's Sermon on the Mount

Chapter 48

Gilbert now has Helen's permission to tell his family her true history which they are delighted to hear. In an aside Gilbert tells of the marriage and happiness of Eliza's elder sister Mary and Jane Wilson's brother Richard, who eventually succeeds Mr Millward as the vicar. Eliza herself marries a wealthy tradesman some time later, but Jane Wilson remains unmarried.

NOTES AND GLOSSARY:
regimen: strict diet

Chapter 49

Helen's letters now describe her husband's worsening condition, caused by a drinking bout in defiance of the doctor's orders. Huntingdon is terrified of death and seems to resent Helen's calm reliance on her faith which he regards as complacency. The wound caused by the fall turns gangrenous, and at last, in great pain and terror, Huntingdon dies. Helen begs her brother to come to her.

NOTES AND GLOSSARY:
flinty: hard
by the Lord Harry: a mild oath, euphemism for 'by the devil'
dip the tip of your finger ... to cool my tongue: a quotation from the story of Dives and Lazarus in the Bible (see Luke 16:24)

Chapter 50

Gilbert now realises that Mrs Huntingdon, the rich widow, is far above him in rank. On Lawrence's return from Huntingdon's funeral he imagines that Helen's brother feels the same about the matter. He decides to wait for the six months they had agreed upon earlier, and then write to her. But just at that time Helen's uncle dies and she goes to stay with her aunt. Gilbert does not know her address, and is reluctant to ask Lawrence.

In another aside Gilbert relates what happened to the people mentioned in Helen's diary. Lady Lowborough eloped to the continent with another lover and died there in poverty and misery some years later. Her husband had divorced her and made a very happy second marriage. Grimsby was killed in a drunken brawl, but Hattersley has kept the promise he had made to Helen, and he and his wife and children live together happily.

NOTES AND GLOSSARY:

afflictive: causing distress

mesalliance: (*French*) marriage with someone of lower rank in society

the unfortunate little Annabella: presumably he suspects that the little girl is not his child, but Huntingdon's

bathos: see note to Chapter 30 above

Chapter 51

Eliza Millward tells Gilbert gleefully that Mrs Huntingdon is going to marry Mr Hargrave, and that Lawrence himself has gone to the wedding. Gilbert starts off at once for Grassdale. He arrives there just as the wedding party is leaving the church. To his joy, the bride and groom are Esther Hargrave and Lawrence himself. Gilbert stops just long enough to wish them joy and then hurries on to Grassdale Manor.

NOTES AND GLOSSARY:

close: secretive

balled: clogged

post-chaise: carriage used for conveying mail and also passengers

gig: a light, two-wheeled carriage

fly: light carriage for hire

favours: knots of ribbon worn at weddings, elections and other occasions

sotto voce: see note to Chapter 18 above

Chapter 52

On his way to the Manor Gilbert learns from the driver of his gig that Hargrave is indeed married, but to a middle-aged, well-to-do lady whom he treats rather unkindly. On arriving at the Manor he finds that Helen has gone to stay with her aunt at Staningley, and he goes in pursuit of her there. On the way he learns that Helen's uncle has left most of his considerable property to Helen, thus making her an even richer woman. Because of this, Gilbert decides to see the house from a distance only and return without even seeing Helen.

NOTES AND GLOSSARY:

after this stir's gotten overed: (*dialect*) when this excitement is over

jointure: property settled on a woman at her marriage, to be hers after her husband's death

a rare long purse: a great deal of money

'The Lightning':   name of a fast coach

hatom: (*dialect*) atom, the smallest part

Chapter 53

By the gates of the house Gilbert meets Helen, her aunt and little Arthur, and is persuaded to come up to the house. After some initial awkwardness Gilbert makes it clear to Helen that it was only her wealth that kept him away, and that he loves her still. Nothing now stands in the way of their happiness. Some months later they are married and settle at Staningley where they have been living happily ever since. Fergus takes over Gilbert's own farm, and Arthur, when grown up, comes to live at Grassdale Manor with his wife, the Hattersleys' daughter Helen.

NOTES AND GLOSSARY:

Linden Grange: the farmhouse attached to the Linden-Car estate

Part 3

Commentary

Plot and structure

Put at its simplest, the purpose of a novel is to tell a story. The author may introduce his main character at a very early stage of his or her life (as in Charles Dickens's (1812–70) *David Copperfield* (1849–50) and *Great Expectations* (1860–1), or in Anne Brontë's other work of fiction, *Agnes Grey*), or he may take up the story at some crucial moment when the main character's whole life is about to be changed, as is the case with *The Tenant of Wildfell Hall*. Whatever the starting point, the story follows the protagonists through their trials and tribulations, and through their happier times as well, to a point where we can see clearly what their future will be, or indeed (as in George Eliot's (1819–80) *Mill on the Floss* (1860)) to the moment of their death.

The simple sequence of events is the plot of the novel, while the way in which these events are arranged and presented gives the novel its structure. About *The Tenant of Wildfell Hall* it could be said that the plot consists of the meeting of Gilbert and Helen, the growth of their love, the misunderstandings and obstacles that separate them and finally of their marriage. Equally it could be said that it is the story of a young girl's disastrous marriage, her attempts to regain her freedom and make a happier life for herself, and of her final success.

Most novels interweave two or more separate plots—indeed it would be hard to find a novel with one single strand of plot alone—but what makes *The Tenant of Wildfell Hall* unusual is the deliberate separation of the two plots. This division gives the novel its structure: it consists of a central part (Helen's diary) which cuts the other part (Gilbert's long letter) into two sections. The central part is the longest (twenty-seven chapters out of fifty-three) and, to the author, the most important.

The separation of the two parts is emphasised by the time element as well: the two letter sections tell of a sequence of events from October 1827 to the summer of 1829, while the central section goes back in time, starting in June 1821 and finishing abruptly in October 1827, roughly where the first section begins.

In other words, the central section is an extremely long flashback*

---

* flashback: a term borrowed from the cinema, meaning a scene from the past, shown by way of explanation or of comment on later events.

into Helen's past history, to which Gilbert's letter serves as a framework, rather like a cumbrous, over-heavy frame for a small, sombre, dramatic painting.

It might as well be admitted that the clumsiness of the structure—further emphasised by the conventional, and here quite unsuitable, division of both the letter part and the diary part into chapters—is the chief weakness of the novel. Given the strong moral purpose of *The Tenant of Wildfell Hall* (of which more will be said in the section of 'Themes', pp.40−6 below), it is clear why Helen's diary, the record of a drunkard's degradation, should be given prominence.

The diary form is also useful in another way: it enables the novelist to describe this degradation with a frankness that would not have been permissible in a straight narrative. Making use of the diary form, with its convention of frankness, still did not save Anne Brontë from critical condemnation for her 'morbid revelling in scenes of debauchery', though to the modern reader it will seem that much has been left to the imagination, presumably on grounds of delicacy ('He himself was ... sick and stupid. I will write no more about that.'—Chapter 31; 'At last, one morning, she entered my chamber with such intelligence that my resolution was taken before she had ceased to speak.'—Chapter 43). The diary form, then, offered to Anne Brontë the chance to say with greater frankness what she had to say about a subject that occupied her mind and filled her heart while she attended her drunken brother.

But what of the other part of the novel, Gilbert's letter? There the moralist stepped aside to make room for the novelist: the author clearly felt a need to introduce an element of suspense into her story. Therefore a narrator was needed who was ignorant of Helen's true history, and who would draw the reader's attention to the mystery surrounding her. There lay the author's difficulty: an impersonal narrator, the author's own voice, is by nature inevitably omniscient, able to see into the minds of the chief characters and read their thoughts (imagine a novel that would tell us nothing about what the people in the story thought, and left it to us to draw what conclusion we could from their actions and conversation alone!). Accordingly Anne Brontë needed another character involved in the story who would tell it as he saw it—in other words she felt she needed another 'I' voice. The absurdity of a diary within another diary being obvious, she settled on the form of a letter.

That her choice was an unfortunate one is clear: why should Gilbert suddenly decide to write to his brother-in-law, Halford, twenty years after the events he is describing, laboriously relating what had happened all those years ago? No explanation is offered, presumably because in the circumstances it is impossible to give a plausible reason. It is asking a good deal of the reader to expect him to accept that a man would sit down and write in instalments a letter a couple of hundred pages long, and in addition include in it a copy of his wife's lengthy diary. Clearly Anne Brontë herself was aware of the intrinsic improbability of including the diary in the letter as she felt the need to offer some kind of explanation:

> I know you would not be satisfied with an abbreviation of [the diary's] contents, and you shall have the whole.... (Chapter 15)

There are indications that, as well as feeling the need to account for the inclusion of the diary in Gilbert's letter, she also wanted to convince her readers that Gilbert really was writing a letter. In the early chapters he repeatedly addresses his brother-in-law in jocular asides, as if to stress the existence of the recipient of the supposed letter:

> I need not tell you that this was my sister Rose .... Nothing told me then, that she, a few years hence, would be the wife of one entirely unknown to me as yet

> Now, Halford, I bid you adieu for the present. This is the first instalment of my debt.   (Chapter 1)

> I perceive with joy ... that ... you desire the continuation of my story ....   (Chapter 2)

> Is it so, Halford? Is that the extent of your domestic virtues, and does your happy wife exact no more?   (Chapter 6)

Gradually, however, Halford fades out of the narrative until Gilbert's letter breaks off to make room for the diary, when Halford is brought in again, to justify this lengthy insertion.

Gilbert's correspondent makes another appearance at the beginning of the second part of the letter ('Well, Halford, what do you think of all this?'—Chapter 45) and at its very close ('We are just now looking forward to the advent of you and Rose'—Chapter 53).

The effect of these reminders, which jolt the reader to remember that he is supposed to be reading a letter, is to stress the artificiality of the device and to expose its irrelevance to the narrative. Reminded frequently of the weakness of the letter form, we are still left wondering about the author's reasons for persisting with such an unsatisfactory structure at all. In the absence of any comments by Anne Brontë herself on the writing of her novel, we can only assume that she wanted an 'I' narrator involved in the story, and in using the quite unnecessary letter frame she was simply following the fashion of her time. We need not look very far for another example of an awkward use of the first-person witness narrator: Emily Brontë's *Wuthering Heights* is a series of eye-witness accounts and diary extracts, with Lockwood providing the linking.

But it seems that Anne Brontë, having decided to use the letter form, soon became absorbed in the telling of the story and forgot about the recipient of the supposed letter, only bringing him back when the break in the narrative, caused by the switch over to the diary, reminded her of her original intention. Most readers will find themselves following her example in this, equally absorbed in the story she had to tell.

If, however, this awkward use of a not altogether satisfactory structural device is a shortcoming in the novelist, surely it is due more to lack of experience in her craft than to lack of talent. After the straight chronological narrative of her first novel, *Agnes Grey*, in *The Tenant of Wildfell Hall* Anne Brontë was attempting a much more ambitious project from the technical point of view.

To begin with, the plot is far more complex. The tale of Helen's unhappy marriage traces not only the sequence of events that led to its failure, but also the changes and developments in the characters of the protagonists. The aim is not only to account credibly for the events described, but also to satisfy the demands of the moral purpose of the novel: it has to act as a warning against temptation.

The element of mystery introduced in the first section has to be maintained first, and then accounted for and elucidated, again credibly. The long flashback in diary form required the introduction of an entirely different background with a new set of characters, to be differentiated—again to some extent with a moral purpose in mind—from the personages of the letter section. And these two sets of people and backgrounds yet had to meet, and be accounted for, at the conclusion of the novel.

There are considerable flaws: the novelist introduces characters into the plot and then finds she has no real use for them. She disposes of them clumsily, settling their future lives in hasty asides, well in advance of the novel's conclusion. She is still learning her craft, writing hastily, not revising enough—and we must be thankful for this, since a rigorous pruning of the novel would surely have deprived us of most of the charming vignettes of village life from Gilbert's diary. The very fact that there was need to prune is proof of abundance. She was a gifted story-teller, with much to tell.

Themes

It can be said that every novel has its theme, its moral. In some novels, such as Jane Austen's (1775–1817) *Pride and Prejudice* (1813) or her *Persuasion* (1818), the theme is never stated explicitly, though the reader may find himself (or, more likely, herself) considering the position of young middle-class women in early nineteenth-century England and contemplating with something like horror the vista of endless boring, idle, useless days that faced these girls at least until or unless they married.

Other novelists state their themes very clearly, using their pen as a weapon in a particular crusade: Charles Dickens is an obvious example, attacking the English legal system, the Poor Law, the educational system, and so on. By her own testimony Anne Brontë belongs to this second category. In her preface to the second edition of *The Tenant of Wildfell Hall*, defending herself against the charges of coarseness and morbid insistence on scenes of debauchery, she says: 'I wished to tell the truth, for truth always conveys its own moral to those who are able to receive it.'

The moral which she wanted to convey, and which forms a major theme in her novel, is that of a tract against alcohol. We may find her abhorrence of alcohol excessive, but we cannot doubt that she is writing in all sincerity, and, moreover, from first-hand experience. The drunkard 'confidentially pushing his head into [Milicent's] face', with 'his face exceedingly flushed' (Chapter 31) is a very realistic picture, and the drunken Grimsby's pompous speech, in which he vainly tries to show just how sober and clear-thinking he is, is reproduced in the same chapter with cruel accuracy.

The link between Branwell Brontë's downfall and early death and Anne's novel is obvious, and has often been pointed out. But there is another theme in the book, of which the reader grows increasingly aware in the course of the diary section. This theme too has links with Anne Brontë's own life, and possibly with another member of her own family, her aunt Miss Branwell. This is the theme of salvation and damnation. Very early in her acquaintance with Arthur Huntingdon Helen already sees him as one on the brink of that fiery pit of hell which seems to have been utterly real to her, and perhaps to Anne Brontë herself. Helen is confident of saving Arthur and sees her marriage to him almost as a religious vocation. When her marriage breaks up and Arthur gives himself up to drink and debauchery, she grows certain of his ultimate damnation.

Hers is a stern God, and when Arthur is dying in pain and terror, she has no comfort to offer him. She is as sure of his damnation as she is— by implication—of her own salvation. We may find such certainties incomprehensible, but they were real enough to Helen, and to Anne Brontë herself. Though in her later years, as her poem 'A Word to the Calvinists' (1843) makes clear, Anne was able to reject the extremist doctrines intellectually, the terror which such an unrelenting faith inspired in her when a little girl under the care of her Methodist aunt, remained vivid in her imagination. All the Brontës were evidently familiar with the Calvinist dogma. Charlotte uses it to stress the harsher side of St John Rivers in *Jane Eyre*, while Emily mocks it in the person of that canting hypocrite, the old servant Joseph in *Wuthering Heights*. Anne alone conveys the terror such a doctrine could inspire in a believer. The dreadful thought of eternal damnation awaiting a sinner such as her brother had been, may have been just as strong a force driving her to write her warning tract in the form of a novel, as Branwell's alcoholism had been.

These twin themes, then, the moral dangers of drink and the spiritual perdition in which it results, are the two explicit messages of *The Tenant of Wildfell Hall*. But throughout the novel another theme makes itself heard more and more strongly, at times by implication, and at other times by direct statement. It is the theme of the position of women in England at this time.

Helen's life history exemplifies several aspects of it. The charming, confident, almost cock-sure young girl changes almost overnight once she is married. Over and over again it is made clear to her that she is legally and socially inferior to her husband. At the time of her marriage, deeply in love, she pays no attention to the question of 'settlements' and thereby ensures her own total financial dependence on her husband. She is treated like a child, incapable of travelling 'alone', that is, accompanied only by her maid and a footman (an ironical foreshadowing of her secret escape later on in the novel, alone with her maid and her child).

It is made clear to her that different moral standards apply to men and women:

> 'The cases are different .... It is a woman's nature to be constant ... but you must have some commiseration for us [men], Helen; you must give us a little more license ....'   (Chapter 27)

After her final break with her husband she must stay with him, and can only escape in secret, as by law her husband could compel her to return to him if he knew her hiding-place.

Too late, she realises the injustices inherent in the sheltered upbringing of young girls, which does nothing to prepare them for the adult world in which they will have to find their way, and does so on grounds which are morally unsound to say the least:

> You think that [a girl] is essentially so vicious, or so feeble-minded that she cannot withstand temptation ... being destitute of real virtue, to teach her how to sin, is at once to make her a sinner, and the greater her knowledge, the wider her liberty, the deeper will be her depravity ....   (Chapter 3)

But she is alone in her awareness of the inequalities and injustices inherent in women's education. Milicent Hattersley, who is treated abominably by her husband, can only submit and weep. Though

Gilbert's sister Rose complains about her mother's preferential treatment of her brothers ('Don't eat so much of that, Rose, Gilbert will like it for his supper . . . . anything will do for the ladies.'—Chapter 6), such protests are part and parcel of amiable family squabbling, and have little bitterness in them beyond the jealousy often found between brother and sister. But the homely sermons on a woman's role, preached by Mrs Markham in Chapter 6, do serve to counterpoint Helen's high expectations of marriage and her subsequent bitter disappointment with its reality. In a curious way Mrs Markham's very practicality is as chillingly effective as Helen's high rhetoric in stressing this third theme of *The Tenant of Wildfell Hall*, which at times overshadows the other two, and yet is never openly acknowledged by the author.

Style

It has to be said at once that Anne Brontë's strength as a novelist does not lie in her style. The plainness of her narrative at times approaches clumsiness, as in Chapter 8: 'put it on (that is, the coat)'. She lacks her sister Charlotte's dramatic eloquence, which turns some parts of *Jane Eyre* and *Villette* into verbal equivalents of an Expressionist painting in which landscape and people are seen as distorted images of the artist's mind. And she has little of Emily Brontë's descriptive powers which leave the reader of *Wuthering Heights* with a lasting memory of the harsh stony moor and its great beauty. Such comparisons will inevitably be made, given the inescapable bracketing together of the Brontë sisters of which readers and critics alike will always be guilty to some extent at least.

Anne Brontë's greatest strength has nothing to do with style or description; it lies in the passionate conviction with which she tells her tale, in the inevitably almost religious fervour with which she discharges her mission. But her writing does rise above the merely competent and has some unique qualities.

Something that will strike most readers once they have reached the diary part of the novel, is the marked difference in style between this section and the two parts of the letter section that encloses it, a difference which is not accounted for by the different sex and circumstances of the narrator.

Gilbert's letter gives a clear, convincing picture of the life in a small North Country village. The Yorkshire background, so powerful in Emily Brontë's *Wuthering Heights*, remains hazy here, but the people and their everyday doings are sharply drawn. Enough detail is given, in descriptions of considerable homely charm, to enable us to visualise the daily round on a prosperous farm, the small pleasures of evening parties, the friendliness, the kindness—and the back-biting and uncharitable gossip—of village society. The dialogue too is authentic, with the sober, pedestrian tones of everyday speech, the family jokes, and the sly innuendos of gossip.

Compare with this genre picture Helen Huntingdon's life as shown in her diary. The stilted unreality of these society people in their amusements, even in their debauchery, offers a marked contrast. Very few details are offered (though such details as we are given are quite accurate—for instance, the rituals of the breakfast table, and of the evening tea-drinking). Arthur Huntingdon himself is drawn clearly enough, but his drinking companions remain shadowy figures, as do the characters on the periphery of the narrative: Esther Hargrave, her mother, even Walter Hargrave. The houses they live in, the parkland they walk in, are yet more shadows.

There are good reasons for this, of course. First of all, the diary form is self-centred almost by definition. A diarist writes for himself, and has no need to describe people and places which are familiar to him. What matters is the effect these people and places have on the writer.

As Anne Brontë chose the diary form deliberately, in order to be able to stress the moral theme (for which Helen Huntingdon is her mouthpiece), it is natural that she should have exploited the conventions of this literary form to the full. She was free to concentrate on Helen, and she used this freedom to discard and ignore more fully, perhaps, than most other writers would; the moralist elbows the novelist aside in this.

There may be another reason why she left the background of Grassdale Manor so dimly sketched and, incidentally, why these society people talk in such an oddly unconvincing, stilted way. She was not writing from her own experience, and had very little material to work from.

In describing the Markhams, the Millwards, and the Wilsons in Gilbert's letter, she was writing about people of a kind she knew well from her own experience of the restricted village society of Haworth. Is it fanciful to suggest that the society at Grassdale Manor is described as if seen by someone on the periphery of that society, who sees them going about their pleasures, but always from a distance, never close enough to listen to their conversation? Someone who attends the breakfast and tea-drinking rituals, sitting some distance away, but who is not included in the dinner party? In other words, the governess? Anne's sister Charlotte is explicit enough about the role of the governess in her description of Mr Rochester's house party in *Jane Eyre*, and Anne's only adult experience of the world outside Haworth—her five years as a governess—was in the same constricted role.

These reasons will go some way to explain the distinctive qualities of the characterisation and description in the two parts of *The Tenant of*

Wildfell Hall. Other characteristics of style cannot so easily be explained by outward circumstances, and their roots must lie in the author herself.

Writing at a time when set descriptive pieces were almost compulsory in a novel, Anne Brontë seems to pay very little attention to this convention. Wildfell Hall itself is described at some length—the semi-derelict old house, the neglected garden with its overgrown topiary—but we have very little impression of the countryside beyond, or of the village. Grassdale Manor, itself a shadow, exists in a shadowy landscape. What we do find is the occasional sharp glimpse from an observing eye, such as 'the last fall of snow was only just wasted away, leaving yet a thin ridge' (Chapter 7), 'the level rays of the sun... displaying patches of semi-transparent leaves of resplendent golden green' (Chapter 9), 'the images [in the water] are partially broken by the sport of aquatic insects' (Chapter 25), 'a shadow suddenly eclipsed the little space of sunshine on the grass before us' (Chapter 29). With the exception of these brief glimpses Anne, who loved to walk on the moors with Emily, keeps her great love largely to herself, unlike her sister. To her, the landscape of the mind, of the emotions, is far more arresting, naturally enough for a novelist with a moral purpose who deals in thoughts and feelings rather than sensations.

The descriptive passages are simple and brief. All the more unexpected are two passages of overt symbolism. In Chapter 33 the game of chess which Helen plays with Hargrave is quite clearly the symbol of the struggle for sexual mastery. In the final chapter of the novel the miraculously undamaged rose from the wintry garden which Helen offers to Gilbert is symbolic of herself, of the suffering through which she has come victorious.

But though Helen loses the chess game, she wins her victory over Hargrave in real life; and Gilbert is so slow to understand that the winter rose brings him Helen's love that she throws it angrily into the snow, and Gilbert has to climb out of the window to rescue it. So it seems that having introduced it, Anne Brontë deliberately rejects the language of symbols in favour of the plain speaking which is her hallmark.

In one respect, however, Anne Brontë's style bears the imprint of her period: occasionally she displays a taste for what to the modern reader seems a crude form of melodrama. The scene between Lawrence and Markham in Chapter 14, with its emphasis on the shedding of blood, the drunken fight in Chapter 31 where Lord Lowborough frees himself by burning Hattersley's hand with a candle, the grisly proofs of Lord Lowborough's struggle against the temptation to commit suicide (Chapter 38), Helen snatching up a palette knife to ward off Hargrave's advances in Chapter 39—all these are the stuff of pure melodrama.

These scenes may seem out of place to us, but if we see *The Tenant of*

Wildfell Hall as Anne Brontë did, as first and foremost a moral tract, their place within the scheme of the novel becomes clear. The Victorian moralist, like the Victorian preacher, knew the value of a dramatic incident to illustrate a sober theme. Despite all this Anne Brontë's 'morbidity' did grate on contemporary sensibility: the relish with which she sets about describing some of these scenes is unexpected, and —except perhaps to the psychologist—inexplicable.

As there is very little high-flown language in the novel (by the standards of her time at any rate), so, at the other end of the scale, there is very little humour. There are a few laboured puns—Boarham/Bore'em, Leighton/Blatant—and there is the mockery with a moral purpose in the tea-drinking scene with the drunken Grimsby. Young Fergus makes a few not very good jokes, entirely in character, but with these few exceptions the general tone is sober, even sombre. If we consider the inspiration behind the writing of the book—to warn against excessive drinking and to direct the reader's thoughts to eternal salvation—this earnestness of tone is of course entirely fitting.

Equally fitting are the frequent biblical references, especially in the diary section, in which the moral and religious content is of paramount importance. But it would be a mistake to see both the echoes of the Bible and the direct quotations as simply a novelist's device. Undoubtedly the main theme of this section—salvation and damnation—led the novelist's thoughts in the direction of the source of her faith, and the language of the Bible offered a natural form of expression for such thoughts, but these days we are apt to forget just how well versed the Victorian novelists and their readers were in the Scriptures. The words of the Bible were introduced and recognised with the unselfconscious ease of long familiarity, and not only by those brought up in a parsonage.

Characterisation

Helen Huntingdon

It has been said that 'Anne Brontë's real strength lies ... in closely following the moral development, the soul-making, of one central character'.* This one character on which she concentrates with some detriment to the other characters in her book, is of course Helen herself, and the observation quoted above is entirely correct.

To some extent, however, this deliberate concentration on the heroine runs counter to the author's conscious purpose. If her intention was to depict the disastrous consequences of drink, in concentrating on Helen she moves beyond the simplicity of a moral tract, for the story of Helen's

---

* I.-S. Ewbank, *Their Proper Sphere*, Arnold, London, 1966, p.84.

marriage as told by herself in her diary more than hints at other causes of its failure apart from Arthur's drinking, some of them inherent in the character of Helen herself. Here the moralist steps aside and the novelist takes over.

In the first part of the novel, when we make Helen's acquaintance through Gilbert's letter, we learn from him that she is beautiful, intelligent, with an independent turn of mind, gifted, a little scornful of other people's views if they differ from her own, and, like many clever people, impatient of small-talk. She condemns the limited and oversheltered upbringing of girls of her class, feeling that it does little to prepare them for the harsher realities of life. More than that, she sees this inadequate education as a reflection of the basic inequalities inherent in society's treatment of men and women.

She has a deep religious faith and high moral principles, and cannot or will not see the virtue of compromise. She seems proud and rather distant in her dealings with the people of the Yorkshire village where she is now living. Gradually we realise that the remoteness and coldness of her behaviour are qualities forced on her by her circumstances; she cannot allow herself to unbend and be friendly as long as she has a secret to keep.

As the author intended, Helen's character develops in depth and breadth in the diary section. In her early discussions with her aunt (Chapters 16–17, 20) Helen's quickness of mind and pert self-confidence serve her well in arguing in favour of Arthur Huntingdon, but gradually the reader becomes uncomfortably aware of an unwillingness to listen to other views that amounts to arrogance. There is, too, a sort of spiritual arrogance in her certainty that she will reform her future husband. Once she has failed in that, she is not prepared to accept him as the man he is, and has been all along—if only she had been willing to see him clearly. The unwillingness to compromise gives her character a hardness, a priggish confidence in being always right, which may have ruined her marriage as much as her husband's drinking.

For one so high-principled and intelligent her choice of husband had been an odd one in the first place: she seems to be quite unaware of her husband as a person, apart from his good looks. His conversation is commonplace, and his vanity very obvious, yet Helen disregards all this—her later bitterness about the upbringing of girls is clearly rooted in her realisation of the folly she herself had committed.

Her religious faith seems deep and sincere, yet she lacks charity: again, there is a quality of arrogance in her contempt for the sinner. It is significant that she is quite unaware of the presumption in dismissing the repentant Hargrave with Christ's words to the woman taken in adultery (Chapter 34).

All through the book we find her clinging to the harsher aspects of

Christianity—the damnation of the sinner rather than the redeeming love. Her letters from Huntingdon's death-bed show her unrelenting in her sense of duty and in her efforts to call her husband to repentance. It is beyond her to hold out to the dying man a hope of salvation if she believes him to be damned.

It is natural that a woman as badly treated by her husband as she undoubtedly had been should feel unforgiving towards him. What seems unpardonable now is her refusal to admit that in her heart she will not forgive the wrongs done to her, and her insistence that Arthur's sins were against God, and that as he is unrepentant, God will not forgive him. Most readers will be aware of more than a sneaking sympathy for the dying man faced with this stern, self-righteous wife.

The character that has emerged by this time is a complex one. Helen's unbending hatred for her husband is balanced by a fiercely possessive love for her little son. She shows kindness and consideration for the servants, and real affection for her loyal old maid Rachel, but her conversation with the distressed Lord Lowborough after his discovery of his wife's adultery betrays more her injured pride than her sympathy with a fellow-sufferer. Perhaps this pride is the key to her character: like that winter rose that had 'stood through hardships none ... could bear' (Chapter 53) she has emerged unbroken but hardened in her faith, her self-respect, her awareness of her own high worth. What has gone from her is softness, gentleness, the ability to demonstrate her affections, to shed easy tears: the girl who wept on hearing Annabella's sad song (Chapter 19) has travelled a long way, along a hard and lonely road.

The question that remains unresolved in studying this complex character is to what extent the contradictions in her nature are of the author's deliberate contrivance. Did Anne Brontë intend Helen to bear some of the responsibility for the failure of her marriage, or did the character of her heroine take on a life of its own, grow fallible and erring like the rest of humanity? Or, without straying too far into the realms of conjecture, has there been quite simply a change in her readers' views on guilt, faith and charity? Each reader will find his or her own answer.

Arthur Huntingdon

The presentation of Huntingdon's character demonstrates the weakness of the diary form. We see him only through Helen's eyes, and although in the early chapters he is described in fairly favourable terms, with emphasis on his good looks and amusing conversation, we soon grow aware of his limitations. He is not particularly intelligent, nor, in spite of his background, well educated, and has very few interests and resources in himself. Like a spoilt child he expects to be amused continuously. His vanity is displayed and commented upon repeatedly; even his many affairs seem to have been conducted largely to gratify his vanity, not his sensuality. Like most vain people of limited intelligence he resents cleverness, particularly in his wife. He is shallow in his affections; having grown tired of his wife he turns to Lady Lowborough, but it is clear that the break-up of his affair with her will be a welcome release for him, as he is growing bored with her as well ('she was so deuced imperious and exacting'—Chapter 38). His boorishness and bad temper are hard to credit, though we have to bear in mind that country gentlemen's manners in the early nineteenth century were pretty rough.

As the diary progresses, however, the reader grows aware of the one-sidedness of the presentation of Huntingdon's character, seen only through the eyes of the injured wife. As the catalogue of his sins and vices lengthens, it becomes increasingly difficult to perceive Hunting-don as a convincing character, alive within the framework of the novel. We see the thick curls and luxuriant whiskers, but the face remains a blank, and the more outrageous his behaviour, the less convinced is the reader of the humanity of this monster.

Oddly, he comes alive in his outbursts when he is dying. His terror of death turns the cardboard monster into a frightened human being, and his peevish yet shrewd criticism of his wife's moral and spiritual super-iority has a convincing ring. All in all, however, having created him as a warning example, Anne Brontë denied Arthur Huntingdon sufficient humanity to make him an entirely successful piece of characterisation.

Gilbert Markham

If the character of Huntingdon suffers by being seen through the eyes of his wife only, Gilbert Markham is never seen at all. With the tearing out of the relevant page in Helen's diary (Chapter 44) we are deprived of even a physical description. We know that he is young and presum-ably handsome, as both Eliza Millward and Helen are attracted to him. He is better educated than most farmers (Chapter 1), intelligent and something of a reader: it is obvious that to the lonely Helen his com-pany and his conversation are a pleasure. He is kind to his mother who spoils him, and kind also to little Arthur even before he becomes inter-ested in his mother. But there is an unpleasant, cruel streak in him also; the description of his attack on Lawrence jars (Chapter 14), as does the sophistry of his self-justification for wishing Arthur Huntingdon dead (Chapter 44).

His treatment of Eliza Millward is unchivalrous and unkind, even if he is provoked by her spite, and his supercilious comments on Eliza's elder sister Mary do little to modify the reader's adverse judgment, while adding to a convincing portrait of the village's most sought-after bachelor. He has been made a little vain by the attentions of the village ladies, and is nettled by Mrs Graham's indifference to him (Chapter 1).

He is proud, independent and rather inclined to take offence. His pride nearly loses him Helen when she becomes an heiress. He has a quick temper; his behaviour to Lawrence and especially his vicious attack on him are proof of this, and his family seem not unaware of the danger of provoking him.

Our curiosity about him can never be entirely satisfied: as the 'I' narrator he reveals himself only indirectly. The reader will continue to wonder about his marriage to Helen, however careful the novelist has been to reassure us on this point ('I need not tell you how happily my Helen and I have lived together, and how blessed we still are in each other's society'—Chapter 53). On the evidence given he seems an inadequate, colourless partner for a woman of her intellectual ability, beauty and talent.

Frederick Lawrence

Lawrence's character suffers from the requirements of the plot. With a secret to keep he does not reveal much of his own character either. Throughout the first part of the letter section the emphasis is on his reserved nature ('Essentially of reserved habits', 'too cold, and shy, and self-contained', 'a certain morbid feeling of delicacy, and a peculiar diffidence'—Chapter 4). His inhibited character is neatly brought out in the comparison to a tight new garment which one 'would fear to split ... by the unrestricted motion of your arms' (Chapter 4 again). There are hints of a lonely, unhappy childhood with a father who was a heavy drinker and something of a recluse, hints which go some way to explain Lawrence's nature. As he and his sister had been brought up separately, no light is shed on his character in Helen's diary.

In the second part of Gilbert's letter, however, Lawrence is presented more fully, as he and Gilbert become friends. He is then shown as somewhat of a self-indulgent dandy, as if compensating by comfort and pleasant surroundings for what is essentially a bleak and lonely life. Not unkindly by nature, he nevertheless will not exert himself overmuch on behalf of others, preferring the role of a passive observer —a characteristic that nearly succeeds in ruining Gilbert's happiness with Helen.

Through this same passivity he might have drifted into marriage with Jane Wilson, except for Gilbert's warning, though the reader may be justified in regarding the affair as of no importance. Having introduced it, the author herself seems to have discarded the theme as superfluous, which it surely is, contributing nothing either to plot or to characterisation. Lawrence's character is essentially defined by the *absence* of any emotional ties, accounted for by his family history; and his marriage to Esther Hargrave, intended to be a surprise to the reader for the sake of the plot of the novel, certainly takes us by surprise in spite of the heavy hints dropped in Helen's letter to Lawrence ('I wish somebody that was worthy to possess her would come and take her away—don't you, Frederick?'—Chapter 49). His marriage surprises because it is so totally out of keeping with the character that the novelist had created.

Rachel

In Rachel Anne Brontë creates with obvious pleasure the archetypal faithful maid, perhaps based on the Brontës' much loved maid, Tabby; dour on the surface, but loyal and full of loving kindness to Helen and her little boy. She had been Helen's nurse, and it is clear that she loves her mistress like her own child. She cannot prevent Helen's disastrous marriage but the hints she drops to her are clear enough. Her North Country voice brings a welcome matter-of-factness into the stilted conversations at Grassdale Manor.

She is no fool, particularly where Helen's welfare is concerned. At Grassdale Manor she protects her by her presence from the unwelcome advances of Walter Hargrave, and at Wildfell Hall she discourages Gilbert's attentions because she is aware of the gossip surrounding her mistress—as well as being full of maternal jealousy. Basically she is a stereotype, but she is a good strong character as well, successfully drawn though lightly sketched.

Lord Lowborough

There is no doubt that Anne Brontë was not at ease with her aristocratic characters: Lord Lowborough is one of the least successful characters in the novel. 'A tall, thin, gloomy man', he seems to have stepped straight out of a moral tract. His life history, as narrated by Huntingdon in Chapter 22, is simply a cautionary tale against the excesses of gambling, drink, and drugs, and there is nothing in either his conversation or his actions that would breathe life into this didactic tale.

Some of the worst excesses of melodrama in *The Tenant of Wildfell Hall* occur in the Lowborough episodes, as if to underline the link between the need to preach a moral lesson and the use of high-coloured illustrations to point to this moral.

Annabella Lowborough

Anne Brontë was more successful with the wicked Annabella Low-borough, stately, tall, handsome, 'too great a flirt to be married' until she captures Lord Lowborough and marries him not for love, but for his title.

Perhaps it needed that spark of feminine malice which such a society lady set off in the author to make the character come alive. Annabella is haughty, contemptuous, amoral, rather used to having her own way, even with her lover Huntingdon for whom she seems to have a genuine passion; she is bored in the company of women ('[she] never likes to waste her musical efforts on ladies' ears alone', as her author remarks through Helen, rather waspishly, in Chapter 19). Her malicious remarks have the knack of making Helen's responses sound priggish. In the confrontation scene between the two women (Chapter 34), Lady Lowborough's uncertain, hesitating words, as she sits 'pressing her finger against her teeth', in contrast to the studied indifference of her pose, come much closer to genuine human utterance than most of the speeches of the other guests, or of her outraged hostess for that matter.

Milicent Hattersley

Milicent is presented as the Victorian ideal of a wife, gentle, child-like (addressed suitably as 'child' by her husband in Chapter 31), small (references are made to her 'little hand' and to 'her tiny foot' in Chapter 32), uncritically devoted to her husband, and a loving mother and sister. Her love for her brother Walter is much stressed and may perhaps account to some extent for her blindness to his real intentions towards Helen. But here, as in her devotion to her husband, she betrays more than unworldliness and innocence. In less charitable eyes there is more than a touch of hypocrisy in this determination to see or hear no evil. Yet she is proved right in her assessment of her husband (Chapter 32): Hattersley does repent, exhorted to do so by Helen in a scene of embarrassing high-mindedness (Chapter 42), and changes his ways and his treatment of his wife.

The reader may well feel a sneaking sympathy for Milicent's husband for having to put up with such determined saintliness (to us, there is more than a whiff of masochism in such odour of sanctity), and agree whole-heartedly with Hattersley's plaintive remark 'when a boy has been eating raisins and sugar-plums all day, he longs for a squeeze of sour orange by way of a change' (Chapter 32).

It is perhaps not correct to say that Anne Brontë has failed with Milicent. She has failed to convince her modern readers at least of Milicent's wholly admirable character, but that is not to say that she has failed to create a character that is all the more convincing perhaps for its ambiguity.

Ralph Hattersley

He is a big man, keen on horses, not very intelligent, a bit of a bore in fact. Boorish in his treatment of his over-meek wife, yet unexpectedly shrewd in his assessment of her, a family man at heart, and not unkind (as may be seen from his concern for the exhausted Helen in Chapter 49 — 'she must have food and sleep, and a mouthful of fresh air now and then . . . . she's worn to a shadow already'): that is about the sum of what we learn about Hattersley. As his function in the novel is to act as a foil to Arthur Huntingdon's greater villainies and a sounding-board for Helen's sermonising, he remains a nebulous figure in himself.

Walter Hargrave

If Hattersley is a cardboard figure, Walter Hargrave is a perplexing problem. That a man of his intelligence, taste and polish should choose his friends among drunken louts such as Grimsby, Hattersley and Huntingdon, is in itself odd. His behaviour towards Helen is even more inexplicable. At times he is kind and understanding, and anxious to spare her feelings, and yet he persists with his unwelcome attentions to her, however, distressed she becomes. It is possible to see in these inconsistencies of his behaviour a reflection of the ambiguities in Helen's own attitude towards him. If she dislikes and distrusts him, why does she choose, for no discernible practical reason, to confide in him her plan of escape? Until the melodramatic incident with the palette knife in Chapter 39, she never repels his advances openly; yet he, allowing for the circumlocutions which the social decencies evidently required, makes his purpose quite plain.

The answer to these perplexities lies perhaps in the moral purpose of the novel. Once we accept the moral theme as over-riding all other considerations, Hargrave's part may be seen quite simply as that of a tempter along Helen's thorny path, and the ambiguities in his character as the result of the conflicting demands of the novelist and the moralist. There are indications that the author was aware of these unresolved ambiguities in Hargrave's character; witness her hasty attempts to blacken him more decisively, such as Esther's report on his harsh behaviour towards her in Chapter 48, and the news of his mercenary marriage and deplorable treatment of his wife in Chapter 52.

Here the moralist takes over from the novelist, and so Hargrave's character remains an unsatisfactory sketch, teasing in what it could have been made into.

Mrs Markham

It has been remarked above (p.44) that Anne Brontë is much more at home in the Yorkshire village than at Grassdale Manor. Clearly it was easier for her to draw her characters in convincing detail against a background which was familiar to her and from which she could take all those convincing details her sharp eye had noticed. Her village personages are drawn with a surer hand, not as characters in a morality play, and are the better for it.

Gilbert's mother is a shrewd, placid lady, a very competent housewife, sure of her wisdom and worth, and consequently a little over-inclined to offer advice to those who seem to her to be in need of it. She is outspoken in her criticism of other people's ways, always excepting the pompous Mr Millward whom she respects and admires quite uncritically, for two very good reasons—he is a man and a clergyman.

She is an indulgent mother to her two sons, especially to Gilbert whom she spoils. Her attitude to him reflects her views on the respective roles of men and women in society. She accepts the conventions of society entirely without reservations, and feels comfortable within them ('in all household matters, we have only two things to consider, first, what's proper to be done, and, secondly, what's most agreeable to the gentlemen of the house—anything will do for the ladies.'—Chapter 6). In this, as in her views on marriage, the upbringing of children, the qualities that constitute an ideal husband (Chapter 6), she is the opposite to Helen Huntingdon, and it is small wonder that it should have taken eight months for her to overcome her prejudice against her daughter-in-law. No doubt she blamed Helen for all the anguish which Gilbert had undergone before his marriage, and which she herself witnessed uncomprehendingly: high passion has no place in her comfortable everyday world.

Fergus and Rose Markham

The part played by Gilbert's brother and sister in the action of the novel is quite a modest one. Fergus's teasing offers us some insights into Gilbert's character, and his convincingly immature humour highlights the petty preoccupations of village society.

Rose's presence serves to enable Gilbert to make Mrs Graham's acquaintance more easily, and to that extent she plays a part in moving the plot forward. Her half-humorous, half-serious complaints on her own subordinate role in the Markham household underscore one of Anne Brontë's major themes in the novel, the position of women in society.

Though both Fergus and Rose are of secondary importance and make only brief appearances in the novel, their creator succeeds in making them come alive. Fergus especially, with his laziness, his huge appetite, clumsy jokes, childish impertinence and constant attempts to draw attention to himself, is a very convincing sketch of a boy in his late teens.

The bright little figure of pretty Rose is not seen very often, but, going about her household duties, fetching the tea-things, making puddings and pies, offering her pert comments on her family, she leaves us with a very clear impression of herself—brisk, cheerful, a little sharp-tongued, happily busy with trivialities.

Mr Millward

Surely Anne Brontë was enjoying herself when she created the Rev. Michael Millward, 'tall, ponderous', with a 'large, square, massive-featured face'. His character is summed up by the author on his first appearance, succinctly but really quite unnecessarily, as she gives her readers ample opportunity to observe the vicar's self-satisfied pomposity, his vanity, intolerance of even a hint of criticism or any opposition to his views, his greediness and love of creature comforts, his uncharitable prejudices.

Every one of his appearances in the novel is an occasion for mockery. At parties he is 'mighty in important dogmas and sententious jokes, pompous anecdotes and oracular discourses' (Chapter 4). When his unsolicited advice is rejected by Gilbert he is 'astounded at such unwonted insolence' and stares 'with a look that plainly said: "What, this to me?"' (Chapter 10). He speaks of his uncalled-for visit to Mrs Graham 'with awful emphasis', using his stick to give weight to his pronouncements (Chapter 11).

Herself a curate's daughter, Anne Brontë is not in the least overawed by the clergy, as her comments on Mr Millward show only too clearly. Perhaps the novelist took over from the moralist here, to relish the cruel mockery, or perhaps, quite to the contrary, the moralist was satirising a clergyman who failed in his pastoral duties? For whatever reason, the satirical portrait of Mr Millward is remarkably successful.

Eliza Millward

The first description we have of her (Chapter 1)—'slight and plump', with a 'gentle and childish' voice, and the manners of 'a pretty playful kitten'—gives little indication of the sly malice of which she is capable, unless we are meant to take a hint from the description of her 'long and narrow eyes'. Apart from her attractive appearance and winning ways she has little to commend her even then as her conversation betrays a trite and shallow mind, preoccupied with gossip and flirtation.

By and by her character changes as she becomes aware of Gilbert's infatuation with Mrs Graham. Petty spite, malicious unfounded gossip and sly innuendos become her hallmark, though she does evoke our sympathy as well, at least to begin with. After all, Gilbert's treatment of her is not kind or chivalrous, especially if we consider their relationship before Mrs Graham's arrival on the scene, and judge it by the standards of the time. However, the author's appeals for sympathy on Eliza's behalf soon cease, and in the second part of Gilbert's letter Eliza plays the part of a potential villainess who would not scruple to betray Helen to her husband out of spite.

Eliza's character is revealed by her speech and actions, and also implicitly by contrast with her elder sister Mary: where Eliza sits 'beautifying' a cambric handkerchief with a deep lace border, her sister is 'absorbed in the hemming of a large, coarse sheet' (Chapter 9).

Mary Millward

As she serves to bring out her sister's character by contrast, so the kind, plain Mary tests the two chief characters of the novel by their reactions to her. In the beginning, Mary Millward is to Gilbert 'little better than a nonentity' (Chapter 9), and when he notices that Mrs Graham likes her company, he at once assumes that this is so, because Helen is a doting mother who will like anyone who is fond of children, and Mary is good with children 'if she is good for nothing else'. This thoughtless, arrogant remark—which might well cause the reader to stop and think about what it betrays about Gilbert's own character—earns a well-merited rebuke from Mrs Graham (Chapter 7). It is indicative of Gilbert's growth to maturity that he too learns to appreciate Mary's real worth (Chapter 48).

Mary's role in the novel, however, is an unimportant one, and she is quite superfluous to the plot. Anne Brontë seems to have realised this, though instead of cutting out this and other irrelevant characters altogether, she simply dispatches them off the page quite early on (Chapter 48).

Mrs Maxwell

Helen's aunt is a severe, humourless, high-principled lady, who loves Helen in her way, but lacks the insight into her ward's character that would make her anxious advice effective. Her own marriage has obviously not been very happy (''"Believe me, matrimony is a serious thing." And she spoke it so seriously, that one might have fancied she had known it to her own cost.'—Chapter 16), but when she tries to impress on Helen the seriousness of marriage, Helen dismisses her warning all the more easily as she feels that her aunt is merely embittered by her own ill luck.

Mrs Maxwell commits a further error of judgment, much graver in its consequences, when she tries to persuade Helen to marry the elderly, worthy but dull Mr Boarham. When Arthur Huntingdon saves her from Mr Boarham's unwelcome attentions, Helen is ready to fall in love with him simply because he is so much younger, more handsome and entertaining than her suitor, and she is not inclined to notice any faults in her deliverer.

In one respect Mrs Maxwell's sermonising is effective: when Helen's marriage fails she does not confide in her aunt or seek her help. Her own pride will not allow her to admit her failure to one who had warned her so sternly, and so she turns instead to her brother and finds a refuge at Wildfell Hall.

In the last part of the novel, however, the widowed Mrs Maxwell, though as hostile to any idea of marriage as ever, seems a much kinder, more affectionate person. Perhaps the death of her husband had softened her, or perhaps she now realises the part her own sternness had unwittingly played in bringing about her niece's disastrous marriage.

Jane Wilson

Though she makes a number of appearances throughout the novel, the handsome and ambitious Jane Wilson is of no real significance. Anne Brontë seems to be aware of this, as she makes no attempt to expand Jane's character beyond the conventional picture of a scheming social climber who hopes to further her own interests and ambitions through marriage. The part of the malicious scandalmonger, which the plot requires, is adequately filled by Eliza on her own, and the ill-feeling between Gilbert and Mr Lawrence, again necessary to advance the plot, is more than adequately fuelled by Gilbert's jealous rage against Lawrence as his rival with Mrs Graham, and does not need Gilbert's tactless warning against Jane to spark it off. Dismissed from the book early, like several other basically superfluous characters, Jane Wilson's real significance for the reader lies in her emphasising Anne Brontë's inexperience in the novelist's craft.

Esther Hargrave

Her part has some significance, both in the plot (the distorted report of her marriage to Lawrence rouses Gilbert to go in search of Helen), and in one of the main themes of the novel, that of the position of women. Like her sister Milicent she is under considerable pressure to marry for money, but unlike her sister she resists until she finds a man she can love. Unlike the younger Helen she gives a good deal of thought to the prospect of marriage and to her choice of partner. Through her, Anne Brontë is able to voice her own indignation at the prospect that awaits a woman who does not marry ('a hanger-on . . . a mere cumberer of the ground'—Chapter 41).

Her character, however, remains rather ill-defined, perhaps because of her youth. We hear of her beauty, intelligence, and high spirits, but there is little in her conversation or her actions to attract or interest (see for instance Chapter 37, where she shows remarkable obtuseness even for an inexperienced girl).

Minor characters

For a novel that concentrates so much on the heroine alone, *The Tenant of Wildfell Hall* offers a considerable range of minor characters: little Arthur Huntingdon, the worldly Mrs Hargrave, the odious and boorish Grimsby, the easy-going Mr Maxwell, Richard and Robert Wilson and their scandal-loving mother, Benson the butler, the dull Mr Boarham, the dissolute old Mr Wilmot. Their numbers are accounted for by the double plot with double sets of personages, but their roles remain unimportant and their characters therefore essentially undeveloped.

Part 4

Hints for study

Studying a novel

It will be necessary to read the novel more than once. Read it for the story first, as the author would have wished you to. During this first reading you will probably form some idea of the novel and identify those aspects of it that might come up for discussion in an examination: its main themes and characters, its structure, the chief character-istics of the author's style.

When you have finished your first reading of the novel, try to find a little time just to think about it. Analyse your own reactions to it now, before you start reading other people's opinions of the novel. Are your reactions to it positive or negative? And why? Did you find yourself arguing with the author or with some of the chief characters during your reading? Make a note of these first emotional reactions; they will be valuable later when you may well find that your ideas on the novel have been shaped by them. But do not fall into the trap of offering your emotional reactions alone, unsupported by analytical thought. Your views do matter; you do not have to agree with what you have read in these Notes or elsewhere, but you have to be clear about your reasons for agreeing or disagreeing.

Now read the novel again, this time more slowly. If the book is your own copy, you might pencil in the margin indications of what makes a particular passage interesting and relevant to further study. (In *The Tenant of Wildfell Hall* it might be C for 'character', S for 'structure', A for 'alcoholism', W for 'position of women', H for 'humour', D for 'description', and so on.)

Keep a notebook handy, and jot down any ideas that occur to you during your reading, always with a page reference. This, especially if you also pencil in markers in the margin, will save you a good deal of time later. Tracking down a quotation to support your argument can be a frustrating and time-consuming business.

During this second reading, use Part 2 of these Notes, especially the detailed summaries which will be a useful check on your own interpret-ation of the action of the novel, while the Notes and Glossary will help you to understand some of the more difficult passages or references.

When you have finished your second reading, go over your notes, arrange them under suitable headings, roughly corresponding to the

categories you have been using for your markers, and read through
what you have written down under each heading. Now try to give these
jottings a shape, linking together ideas that follow on from one
another, or that support each other.

For instance, under 'Structure' you may have made a note about the
structure of the novel, about the central part being cast in the form of a
diary. Under 'Character' you may have noted the flatness of the sup-
porting characters at Grassdale Manor. The diary form, concentrating
on the diarist herself and, to a lesser extent, on her husband, does not
allow for analysis of the other characters, seen only in so far as they
affect the writer of the diary, and here lies the reason for their defect-
ive characterisation.

This exercise is a very useful part of your preparatory work. Without
attempting a full-length essay at this stage, you will find that writing
down your ideas in some sort of order will clarify your thoughts and let
your view of the novel take shape.

When you have given yourself time to formulate your own views, do
a double check. First read Part 3, Commentary, in these Notes, not to
check whether you were right, but to see whether you can establish and
maintain your own views even if they differ from someone else's.

For the second part of your double check, read the novel again, or at
least go over it to see whether your own ideas on the novel can be sup-
ported by references to the text. You may well find that your memory,
even after two readings, has played tricks on you (we all tend to rewrite
in our heads the books we have read). Some of your ideas may have to
be modified accordingly.

Quotations

Mention was made above of references to the text, to support your
opinions. This brings us to the question of quotations, which can offer
some difficulties when it comes to a novel. Unlike poetry or drama
(where suitable, easily memorised quotations seem to leap from the
page), finding quotations of manageable length in a novel is not so
easy. Yet examiners do regard quotations as proof of your knowledge
of the prescribed text. The best way out of the difficulty is to think
about the novel and decide which of its aspects are most likely to come
up for discussion in essay questions, and then go over the text quickly
to find quotations which would bear out your views on likely questions. Here the pencilled markers you have made in the margin will
prove useful, but remember to keep your quotations short. You must
quote accurately, and your memory may not be at its best under stress.

To give an example, in a novel like *The Tenant of Wildfell Hall* the
position of women in the early nineteenth century may well form the

subject of an essay question, and there are several passages in the novel which could be quoted in support of the view that Anne Brontë was fully conscious of the unjust treatment of women. (Some of these passages are briefly mentioned in the first specimen essay below, but you might find it a useful exercise now to try to find suitable quotations for an essay of this kind.)

But however valuable quotations are, they can be dangerous too: never try to build your answer round a quotation you happen to have learnt. You must always answer the question, or discuss the topic, as given in the essay title; you must formulate your views first on the basis of a thorough knowledge of the novel as a whole, and then, and only then, support them by suitable quotations.

Planning your essay

When preparing for an examination, find out how many questions you will be expected to answer, and how much time you will have. Work out the time allotted to each question, remembering to allow time for checking your answers.

It will obviously be useful practice to attempt to answer an essay question from the list of specimen questions on p.62. Simulate as much as possible the examination-room conditions (a fixed time limit for your answer, no text to help you with the quotations). Start timing yourself *before* you decide which of the specimen questions you will answer.

Once you have decided which question you are going to answer, jot down your arguments for or against (or both; it is perfectly reasonable to offer a balanced view of both sides of the question). Now you can start on your essay.

First, a brief introduction. This should sum up the basic theme of the essay, and indicate the line you are going to take in discussing it.

Second, your arguments, point by point, with references to the novel, either quotations or references to particular scenes and characters. Any such references must be strictly relevant to the point you are making: simply retelling the plot is no answer at all.

Take care not to indulge in generalisations beyond the scope of the novel. For instance, you may draw your own conclusions about Anne Brontë's views on the position of women, but they must be based on the views she actually expresses in the novel, through one of her characters. Then it is up to you to decide whether these were views she herself shared, and to show how, through reading the novel and thinking about it, you formed your conclusions.

Third, a summing up which briefly recapitulates the second part of the essay, your view of the problem raised in the essay question.

Specimen questions

(1) 'She is a moralist first and a woman second' (I.-S. Ewbank, *Their Proper Sphere*, p.85)—do you agree with this assessment of Anne Brontë?

(2) 'I wished to tell the truth, for truth always conveys its own moral to those who are able to receive it.' To what extent is the moral to which Anne Brontë refers still conveyed to her readers today?

(3) From reading the novel, what picture can you form of the day-to-day life at Grassdale Manor and at Linden-Car?

(4) Would you agree that Anne Brontë's strength lies in 'closely following the moral development, the soul-making' (I.-S. Ewbank, *Their Proper Sphere*, p.84) of one central character?

(5) Which aspects of *The Tenant of Wildfell Hall* as a novel are affected by Anne Brontë's choice of the letter and diary form?

(6) Consider the character of Arthur Huntingdon; does it change and develop in the course of the novel?

(7) Taking *The Tenant of Wildfell Hall* as a novel with a message, what would you say is its message and how is it conveyed?

(8) Chart the changes in the relationship between Helen and her husband by selecting some five or six crucial incidents.

(9) Consider which of the secondary characters have a significant part to play in the novel.

(10) Do you think the form of *The Tenant of Wildfell Hall* is essential to the message its author was so anxious to convey?

Specimen answers

(2) 'I wished to tell the truth, for truth always conveys its own moral to those who are able to receive it.' To what extent is the moral to which Anne Brontë refers still conveyed to her readers today?

In order to answer the question posed by the title of this essay we must decide, first, what the moral was which Anne Brontë wished to convey in her novel, and, second, whether present-day readers will interpret her novel in the way she had intended, or whether they will see it in a different light.

According to her sister Charlotte, Anne Brontë decided to write *The Tenant of Wildfell Hall* as a warning against the evil effects of drink which she had witnessed at first hand in the degradation, through alcohol and drugs, of her brother Branwell.

As she was convinced that telling the unvarnished truth about the effect of excessive drinking would convey her message, she took trouble to chart the disintegration of Arthur Huntingdon in detail.

Through undoubtedly she, like her sisters, had a liking for what might now be described as melodrama, her use of it in the drunken scenes at Grassdale Manor was motivated by her need to show drinking as abhorrent and degrading.

Today's readers will recognise in her detailed descriptions a very modern perception of drink as an addiction, almost a disease. (Arthur complains of having 'an infernal fire in [his] veins' early in the novel, and of 'This cursed thirst' when he is dying.) Though Anne Brontë dwells on the physical aspects of alcoholism in some detail, this degradation of the body is not her main theme. As alcoholism is to her a vice, the physical decay matters less to her than the moral degradation that goes with it, and the loss of divine grace—in other words, damnation. The 'cursed thirst' is only a foretaste of the fires of hell, which seemed to be so real to Helen. The scene in which the dying Arthur imagines Helen, like Job in the Bible, refusing even to dip the tip of her finger in water to cool his tongue while he is suffering the torments of hell, is one that was undoubtedly familiar to church-goers from innumerable sermons.

For modern readers, however, this message of the novel has lost its weight and urgency. While we accept the facts of the degrading physical and mental effects of alcoholism, we may be inclined to regard the alcoholic as a sick man rather than a sinner. The fact that Anne Brontë was not unaware of this medical aspect of alcoholism and yet felt compelled to condemn it so vehemently, indicates how strong the moralist in her was. The reason why she took so strong a moral view of alcoholism has already been indicated: physical decay went hand in hand with moral decay, with fall from grace and therefore with damnation. We know from Anne Brontë's life story and from her poems that since her childhood she was preoccupied with the twin questions of salvation and damnation, and though in later life she arrived at an altogether gentler interpretation of the Gospel's message as one of mercy and love, the terrors of eternal damnation obviously remained real in her artistic imagination even if they receded from her religious faith.

This ultimate message of *The Tenant of Wildfell Hall*, however, is one that is even more difficult for the modern reader to accept. In our present climate of religious doubt there is no certainty of either salvation or damnation, and Anne Brontë's vision of hell, realistically painted in flames, appears almost naïve to an age that would probably believe more readily in the hell of Jean-Paul Sartre's (1905–80) *Huis Clos* (1943)—a place where the dead go on re-living forever in bitterness and sadness their own lives.

However, even if the moral and religious message of *The Tenant of Wildfell Hall* has lost some of its impact for today's readers, the novel conveys another message to us with a force perhaps unforeseen and unintended by its author. This is the author's indignation at the unjust treatment of women. To present-day readers, women especially, the fact that a drunken husband could make it legally and materially impossible for his wife to escape from his brutal treatment, may arouse far stronger emotions than any description of his drunken behaviour. Anne Brontë takes a wider view of the matter, going beyond the legal injustices inflicted on married women by depriving them of legal and financial independence, to the basic question of society's attitude to women. She rightly points out that girls' upbringing did nothing to prepare them for the harsh realities of the world they would enter upon marriage. Sweeping aside the platitudes about preserving innocent girlhood, she sees the basic inequality of sexes reflected in an attitude that condemns a woman for a single wrong step while applauding the same action in a man as in some way strengthening him and making him a better man. She contrasts Arthur Huntingdon's arrogant 'The cases are different . . . . It is a woman's nature to be constant' (Ch. 27) with Helen's bitter 'they [men and women] are both weak and prone to err, and the slighest error . . . will ruin the one, while the character of the other will be strengthened and embellished' (Ch. 3), while Rose Markham's half-joking, half-angry 'anything will do for the ladies' (Ch. 6) echoes the charge of injustice on an altogether more trivial, everyday level.

The conventional view of marriage, summed up so arrogantly by Arthur Huntingdon and attacked so bitterly by his wife, is exemplified yet again in the characters of Ralph Hattersley and his wife Milicent. While Hattersley is a paler, milder version of Arthur Huntingdon, his docile, passive wife offers a complete contrast to Helen. Where Milicent weeps and suffers uncomplainingly, Helen accuses and protests, and, once she has realised that her marriage has failed disastrously and irremediably, sets about fighting her way out of the prison in which law and society conventions have placed her. The reader may well wonder whether the not altogether convincing reformation of Hattersley and the happiness this brings to his wife and family and ultimately to himself, was not a concession to Anne Brontë's reading public, granted all the more readily because the novelist had by then discharged her duty as a moralist.

To sum up, then, there is no simple yes-or-no answer to the question posed by the title of this essay. In her novel Anne Brontë succeeded in conveying the simple moral of the disastrous consequences of succumbing to the temptations of alcohol, but to her readers today her moral is perhaps less crucial than her diagnosis of the underlying cause of the unhappiness which her marriage brought to Helen. The obvious reason why her marriage came to grief—because her husband was a drunkard—matters less, in the final analysis, than the fact that legally and conventionally she was expected to bear the misery of her life, having been educated and conditioned to accept this or any other misery which her husband chose to inflict upon her.

In the light of this reinterpretation of the message of *The Tenant of Wildfell Hall* Anne Brontë's declaration that 'truth always conveys its own moral' acquires a new, deeper meaning.

---

(10) Do you think the form of *The Tenant of Wildfell Hall* is essential to the message its author was so anxious to convey?

In order to answer the question posed here we shall need first to define the form, that is, the structure of the novel, and what its distinguishing characteristics are, and define also the message conveyed by the novel. Only then shall we be able to decide whether the form is essential to the message.

The structure of *The Tenant of Wildfell Hall* is unusual. It consists of an unbelievably long letter, written by the young hero, Gilbert Markham, to tell his brother-in-law about the events which had taken place twenty years earlier, and which led to his happy marriage to Helen Huntingdon. Inserted in the letter is a copy of the diary written by Gilbert's wife, relating the story of her disastrous first marriage to an alcoholic, and her life up to the time when she met Gilbert. The diary is the longest and clearly the most important part of the novel.

Because both the letter and the diary are written in the first person, both offer us the narrator's (be it the letter-writer's or the diarist's) point of view only, and we never learn what the other people in the novel are thinking and feeling, unless they describe their thoughts and feelings in conversation in the narrator's presence. Even then we receive only second-hand accounts, inevitably coloured by the narrator's reactions and interpretations.

So much for the form. The message which Anne Brontë wished to convey in her novel was a warning against the evils of alcohol. We have it on her sister Charlotte's authority that Anne was very deeply affected by witnessing the decline and early death through alcoholic addiction of her brother Branwell, and that she felt it her duty to warn others of the dangers of drink. It should perhaps be stressed here that in Anne Brontë's eyes the physical and mental degradation through alcoholism leads inevitably to spiritual degradation as well—in other words to perdition and eternal damnation. This conviction gives the novel its intensity of feeling, and makes the need to preach in order to convince and save from sin and damnation an imperative necessity, indeed a duty.

If we bear in mind that the book was written almost in a spirit of missionary fervour, we perceive then that its form was chosen deliberately.

Of course, both letter and diary were popular forms in fiction, but it seems clear that Anne Brontë chose to use them both in one novel, in spite of the technical difficulties in accounting for them credibly, exactly because, as was remarked above, both these forms offer one person's view of the events described.

What might be seen as weakness in the narration, the narrowness of vision, becomes its strength if used precisely to convey one moral vision, all the more intense because narrow. We are not allowed to see into Arthur Huntingdon's heart, to know what made him turn to alcohol and literally drink himself to death: therefore we should be able to condemn him outright, as we have no mitigating evidence to consider.

In other words, the form chosen, particularly the diary in which the writer is permitted to express her own views alone, coloured by her suffering and indignation, enables the novelist to state her case against alcoholism in the strongest terms possible. A moral tract would never be as effective as a work of fiction, written in a form which allows the novelist to appeal to the reader's imagination and feelings to far better effect.

However, this argument does not apply quite so well to the letter section of the novel. In this section there is far less need for the first-person narrative to convey the moral message. After all, the letter form simply provides a framework for the diary section which is the heart of the novel, and of the novelist's message.

What the letter form does provide is a narrator who is as intrigued by the mysterious Mrs Graham as we are, and as ignorant of her life history. In other words, the letter section serves to create and maintain an atmosphere of mystery, to hold the reader's interest until the revelations of the diary.

To sum up: the form of the novel serves its moral purpose most effectively in the central diary section. The letter section, less successful technically, nevertheless maintains our interest in the novel as a work of fiction—and perhaps by making us wish to know more about Helen Graham disposes us to read her diary with sympathy and compassion and so to receive the novel's message more readily. To that extent it too serves the author's purpose, however indirectly.

Part 5

Suggestions for further reading

The text

BRONTË, ANNE: *The Tenant of Wildfell Hall*, Zodiac Press, Chatto and Windus, London, 1954.

BRONTË, ANNE: *The Tenant of Wildfell Hall/Agnes Grey*. Introduction by Margaret Lane, Everyman's Library, Dent, London, 1958. (Also available in paperback.)

BRONTË, ANNE: *The Tenant of Wildfell Hall*. Introduction by Phyllis Bentley, Panther/Granada, London, 1969 (paperback).

BRONTË, ANNE: *The Tenant of Wildfell Hall*. Introduction by Winifred Gérin, ed. by G.D. Hargreaves, Penguin English Library, Penguin Books, Harmondsworth, 1979 (paperback).

Other works by Anne Brontë

BRONTË, ANNE: *Agnes Grey*. In *The Tenant of Wildfell Hall/Agnes Grey*. Introduction by Margaret Lane, Everyman's Library, Dent, London, 1958. (Also available in paperback.)

BRONTË, ANNE: *The Poems of Anne Brontë*, with a commentary by Edward Chitham, Macmillan, London, 1979. With a stimulating introduction linking Anne Brontë's poems to events in her life.

Biography

GÉRIN, WINIFRED: *Anne Brontë*, Allen Lane, London, 1976. The only comprehensive biography available.

A good deal of information about Anne Brontë may of course be found in works dealing with her sisters, individually or jointly:

BENTLEY, PHYLLIS: *The Brontës and Their World*, Thames & Hudson, London, 1969. Valuable for the many excellent illustrations.

GASKELL, ELIZABETH: *Life of Charlotte Brontë*. Introduction by Winifred Gérin, Everyman's Library, Dent, London, 1971. This famous biography, first published in 1857, by a woman novelist who knew Charlotte, makes interesting reading, even if it is now regarded as not entirely reliable.

GÉRIN, WINIFRED: *The Brontës*, 2 vols., Writers and Their Work Series, Longman for the British Council, London, 1973—4. Brief but informative, with excellent bibliographies. The first volume deals with their lives, the second with their work.

Criticism

CRAIK, W.A.: *The Brontë Novels*, Methuen, London, 1968. Contains a chapter on *The Tenant of Wildfell Hall*.

EWBANK, INGA-STINA: *Their Proper Sphere*, Arnold, London, 1966. A discussion of the Brontës as women novelists, from a feminist stance.

STEVENSON, W.H.: *Emily and Anne Brontë*, Profiles in Literature Series, Routledge and Kegan Paul, London, 1968. Intended for the general reader. Brief introduction, followed by extracts chosen to illustrate the essential differences between the two writers in structure, technique, style and background of ideas.

WINNIFRITH, TOM: *The Brontës*, Masters of World Literature Series, Macmillan, London, 1977. Brief summaries of the lives of the sisters, followed by discussion of their juvenilia, their poetry and their novels. Makes some useful points on the dangers of the biographical approach to their work.

The author of these notes

HANA SAMBROOK was educated at the Charles University in Prague and the University of Edinburgh. She worked as an editor in educational publishing and was for some years on the staff of the Edinburgh University Library. She now works as freelance editor in London.

York Notes: list of titles

CHINUA ACHEBE
A Man of the People
Arrow of God
Things Fall Apart

EDWARD ALBEE
Who's Afraid of Virginia Woolf?

ELECHI AMADI
The Concubine

ANONYMOUS
Beowulf
Everyman

JOHN ARDEN
Serjeant Musgrave's Dance

AYI KWEI ARMAH
The Beautyful Ones Are Not Yet Born

W. H. AUDEN
Selected Poems

JANE AUSTEN
Emma
Mansfield Park
Northanger Abbey
Persuasion
Pride and Prejudice
Sense and Sensibility

HONORÉ DE BALZAC
Le Père Goriot

SAMUEL BECKETT
Waiting for Godot

SAUL BELLOW
Henderson, The Rain King

ARNOLD BENNETT
Anna of the Five Towns

WILLIAM BLAKE
Songs of Innocence, Songs of Experience

ROBERT BOLT
A Man For All Seasons

ANNE BRONTË
The Tenant of Wildfell Hall

CHARLOTTE BRONTË
Jane Eyre

EMILY BRONTË
Wuthering Heights

ROBERT BROWNING
Men and Women

JOHN BUCHAN
The Thirty-Nine Steps

JOHN BUNYAN
The Pilgrim's Progress

BYRON
Selected Poems

ALBERT CAMUS
L'Etranger (The Outsider)

GEOFFREY CHAUCER
Prologue to the Canterbury Tales
The Franklin's Tale
The Knight's Tale
The Merchant's Tale
The Miller's Tale
The Nun's Priest's Tale
The Pardoner's Tale
The Wife of Bath's Tale
Troilus and Criseyde

ANTON CHEKHOV
The Cherry Orchard

SAMUEL TAYLOR COLERIDGE
Selected Poems

WILKIE COLLINS
The Moonstone
The Woman in White

SIR ARTHUR CONAN DOYLE
The Hound of the Baskervilles

WILLIAM CONGREVE
The Way of the World

JOSEPH CONRAD
Heart of Darkness
Lord Jim
Nostromo
The Secret Agent
Victory
Youth and *Typhoon*

STEPHEN CRANE
The Red Badge of Courage

BRUCE DAWE
Selected Poems

WALTER DE LA MARE
Selected Poems

DANIEL DEFOE
A Journal of the Plague Year
Moll Flanders
Robinson Crusoe

CHARLES DICKENS
A Tale of Two Cities
Bleak House
David Copperfield
Great Expectations
Hard Times
Little Dorrit
Nicholas Nickleby
Oliver Twist
Our Mutual Friend
The Pickwick Papers

EMILY DICKINSON
Selected Poems

JOHN DONNE
Selected Poems

THEODORE DREISER
Sister Carrie

GEORGE ELIOT
Adam Bede
Middlemarch
Silas Marner
The Mill on the Floss

T. S. ELIOT
Four Quartets
Murder in the Cathedral
Selected Poems
The Cocktail Party
The Waste Land

J. G. FARRELL
The Siege of Krishnapur

GEORGE FARQUHAR
The Beaux Stratagem

WILLIAM FAULKNER
Absalom, Absalom!
As I Lay Dying
Go Down, Moses
The Sound and the Fury

HENRY FIELDING
Joseph Andrews
Tom Jones

F. SCOTT FITZGERALD
Tender is the Night
The Great Gatsby

E. M. FORSTER
A Passage to India
Howards End

ATHOL FUGARD
Selected Plays

JOHN GALSWORTHY
Strife

MRS GASKELL
North and South

WILLIAM GOLDING
Lord of the Flies
The Inheritors
The Spire

OLIVER GOLDSMITH
She Stoops to Conquer
The Vicar of Wakefield

ROBERT GRAVES
Goodbye to All That

GRAHAM GREENE
Brighton Rock
The Heart of the Matter
The Power and the Glory

THOMAS HARDY
Far from the Madding Crowd
Jude the Obscure
Selected Poems
Tess of the D'Urbervilles
The Mayor of Casterbridge
The Return of the Native
The Trumpet Major
The Woodlanders
Under the Greenwood Tree

L. P. HARTLEY
The Go-Between
The Shrimp and the Anemone

NATHANIEL HAWTHORNE
The Scarlet Letter

SEAMUS HEANEY
Selected Poems

ERNEST HEMINGWAY
A Farewell to Arms
For Whom the Bell Tolls
The African Stories
The Old Man and the Sea

GEORGE HERBERT
Selected Poems

HERMANN HESSE
Steppenwolf

BARRY HINES
Kes

HOMER
The Iliad

ANTHONY HOPE
The Prisoner of Zenda

GERARD MANLEY HOPKINS
Selected Poems

WILLIAM DEAN HOWELLS
The Rise of Silas Lapham

RICHARD HUGHES
A High Wind in Jamaica

THOMAS HUGHES
Tom Brown's Schooldays

ALDOUS HUXLEY
Brave New World

HENRIK IBSEN
A Doll's House
Ghosts
Hedda Gabler

HENRY JAMES
Daisy Miller
The Europeans
The Portrait of a Lady
The Turn of the Screw
Washington Square

SAMUEL JOHNSON
Rasselas

BEN JONSON
The Alchemist
Volpone

JAMES JOYCE
A Portrait of the Artist as a Young Man
Dubliners

JOHN KEATS
Selected Poems

RUDYARD KIPLING
Kim

D. H. LAWRENCE
Sons and Lovers
The Rainbow
Women in Love

CAMARA LAYE
L'Enfant Noir

HARPER LEE
To Kill a Mocking-Bird

LAURIE LEE
Cider with Rosie

THOMAS MANN
Tonio Kröger

CHRISTOPHER MARLOWE
Doctor Faustus
Edward II

ANDREW MARVELL
Selected Poems

W. SOMERSET MAUGHAM
Of Human Bondage
Selected Short Stories

J. MEADE FALKNER
Moonfleet

HERMAN MELVILLE
Billy Budd
Moby Dick

THOMAS MIDDLETON
Women Beware Women

THOMAS MIDDLETON *and* WILLIAM ROWLEY
The Changeling

ARTHUR MILLER
Death of a Salesman
The Crucible

JOHN MILTON
Paradise Lost I & II
Paradise Lost IV & IX
Selected Poems

V. S. NAIPAUL
A House for Mr Biswas

SEAN O'CASEY
Juno and the Paycock
The Shadow of a Gunman

GABRIEL OKARA
The Voice

EUGENE O'NEILL
Mourning Becomes Electra

GEORGE ORWELL
Animal Farm
Nineteen Eighty-four